Teachable Moments *has given me a fr* *a charming book with a happy balanc* *There are insights about a range of subjec... ....u..... ....u, contemplative* *prayer, and the devil. Johnny White is a shrewd and realistic observer of life in and outside the church today. Each chapter in the book is short and ends with meaningful questions that can be used for personal reflection or group discussion. I recommend it enthusiastically to anyone who wishes to be guided in life by the spiritual wisdom of Jesus our Lord.*

FISHER HUMPHREYS
PROFESSOR OF DIVINITY, EMERITUS
SAMFORD UNIVERSITY
BIRMINGHAM, ALABAMA

For those of us for whom the Lord's Prayer has become overly familiar, Johnny White recovers the radical message of the prayer of Jesus: that God is the loving Father of every human being. His new book is a rich mixture of pastoral reflection, scholarly analysis, church history, popular culture, and personal experiences from his own life. The successive chapters consider the nine petitions of the prayer and end with provocative questions that move us from mere reflection to the actual practice of prayer. Thank you, Johnny!

DANIEL B. CLENDENIN, PHD
WWW.JOURNEYWITHJESUS.NET
"A WEEKLY WEBZINE FOR THE GLOBAL CHURCH"
PALO ALTO, CALIFORNIA

Everyone needs help with prayer. This great little book on the Lord's Prayer will surely be of great use to many people—it is thoughtful, easy to read, and peppered with good illustrations. I recommend it!

IAIN PROVAN
MARSHALL SHEPPARD PROFESSOR OF BIBLICAL STUDIES
REGENT COLLEGE
VANCOUVER, CANADA

This is a wonderful companion book and a great "travelers guide" to the Lord's Prayer. Each chapter has guide stones of scripture, story and personal reflection. Johnny White has taken the reader on a pilgrimage into the concepts revealed in the prayer, stopping to savor and breathe making the journey sacred and enabling.

SUZII PAYNTER
EXECUTIVE COORDINATOR (RETIRED)
COOPERATIVE BAPTIST FELLOWSHIP
ATLANTA, GEORGIA

Johnny,
God alone knows the power of your gentle and pastoral leadership style. Nonetheless, I believe your presence has been most critical in the health and life of the church. Above all, thanks for the gift of friendship.

CALVIN MILLER
POET, PASTOR, PROFESSOR, AND FRIEND
NOVEMBER 2001

TEACHABLE MOMENTS

Baine,

Lifelong friends are the
best kind of friends!

J White

2022

P.S. "cure for insomnia"

TEACHABLE MOMENTS

Theological Reflections from
The World's Most Familiar Prayer

Johnny White

ELM HILL

A Division of
HarperCollins Christian Publishing

www.elmhillbooks.com

© 2019 Johnny White

Teachable Moments

Theological Reflections from
The World's Most Familiar Prayer

Published in Nashville, Tennessee, by Elm Hill, an imprint of Thomas Nelson. Elm Hill and Thomas Nelson are registered trademarks of HarperCollins Christian Publishing, Inc.

Elm Hill titles may be purchased in bulk for educational, business, fund-raising, or sales promotional use. For information, please e-mail SpecialMarkets@ ThomasNelson.com.

Library of Congress Cataloging-in-Publication Data

Library of Congress Control Number: 2019909410

ISBN 978-1-400327294 (Paperback)
ISBN 978-1-400327300 (Hardbound)
ISBN 978-1-400327317 (eBook)

DEDICATION

Pat Coventry
Prayer Ministry Coordinator
Trinity Baptist Church
San Antonio, TX

Martha Greer
Prayer Ministry Coordinator
The Church at Horseshoe Bay
Horseshoe Bay, TX

Patricia White
Most cherished prayers
for nearly fifty years!

TABLE OF CONTENTS

*"He has made everything
beautiful in its time.
He has also set eternity
in the human heart;
yet no one can fathom
what God has done
from beginning to end."*
ECCLESIASTES
chapter 3 verse11

WHY PRAY?

Have you noticed? Jesus never bothered to argue or debate the existence of God. He assumed it. Neither did He argue or debate the validity of prayer. He just did it. Many will disagree, but I believe that even those who do not believe in God will reach out to God at certain times under certain circumstances. Prayer is inevitable.

My all-time favorite television sitcom was *All in the Family.* Those loveable characters—Archie and Edith Bunker; their daughter, Gloria; and their Polish son-in-law, Michael Stivic (not so affectionately called the Meathead); all of them plus their African American neighbors, the Jeffersons—were the *exaggerated caricatures* of who we were as a nation during the 1970s. They were the ultimate satire on the generation gap, the gender gap, the education gap, the political gap, the ethnicity gap, and the religion gap. They were a huge precursor of today's pluralistic divisions.

In my all-time favorite episode, the Bunker family was sitting at the dining table when Archie, as usual, made some outrageously prejudicial comment. Michael, the Meathead, jumped from the table waving his arms in the air and yelled: *"Archie, when you say things like that—I thank God I'm an atheist."*

The camera immediately switched to Archie's face and caught that familiar smirk, and then panned to Michael's face which registered his realization of the ultimate self-contradiction: *I thank God I'm an atheist.* And in that moment, I suspect we learned something important about Norman Lear, the observant yet agnostic Jewish creator of *All in the Family.*

That self-contradictory statement points to a truth about our human nature: whether one believes in God or not, there are occasions when every person talks to God *as if* God exists. Or we talk to ourselves as if we *are* god.

It seems that we have an innate need to reach out beyond ourselves for *something more,* to talk privately and confidentially to *Someone* (even if only talking to ourselves).

There are exhilarating moments in life that create a desire to give thanks to *Someone* for things undeserved and unexplainable. But to Whom do you express that feeling of gratitude?

There are crisis moments in life when, without prior thought or intention, we cry out to God for help or intervention. But to whom do you cry out? And unfortunately, there are also tragic times in life when we have the insatiable need to plead on behalf of those we love. But with Whom do you plead?

The renowned Harvard scholar, William James, wrote a famous book over 100 years ago that has stood the test of time. In his book, *Varieties of Religious Experience,* an early psychological study of religious experience, Dr. James draws the conclusion: *"We cannot help praying."*

The need to pray exists regardless of whether you believe

humankind created God out of a sense of need or whether you believe along with the writer of Ecclesiastes that the Creator God has *"set eternity in the hearts of men."* Even those who are agnostic or atheistic will, in a time of crisis, automatically reach out in prayer.

As the great French mathematician and philosopher, Blaise Pascal, reportedly said: *"There is a God-shaped vacuum in every human heart."* In times of crisis, we will pray. Even Jesus knew the emotion of this kind of prayer. In the Garden of Gethsemane just before his betrayal and arrest, he prayed fervently, even desperately, to the point of sweating drops of blood, *"Let this cup pass from me."*

Having debated with myself for many years about the efficacy of prayer to change circumstances and after reading innumerable books on prayer over many years, I have concluded (as others before me) that there is one overwhelmingly valid reason to cultivate a habit of prayer. The supreme argument that we should pray is simply this: Jesus prayed.

Before Jesus ever said anything about how or what to pray, he first demonstrated the priority of prayer in his own life. And if Jesus needed to pray, for whatever reason, then we must need to pray as well. From a pragmatic, practical point of view, praying is a spiritually, emotionally, and physically beneficial practice. It causes one to slow down and think about ultimate things rather than go through life in a trivial way.

One way to think about the life and words of Jesus is this: Jesus came to show us what God is really like and correct all our misconceptions about God. In this brief familiar prayer that we repeat all too casually, Jesus does just that. He reveals what God is really like and how he desires for us to relate to God.

> *"Jesus came to show us what God is really like and correct all our misconceptions about God."*

For Personal Reflection or Group Interaction

How do you respond to the assertion that we cannot help but pray? Do you agree that atheists pray?

Do you believe prayer changes circumstances? Have there been experiences in your life where you believe this has happened?

What do you think Jesus prayed about? Did he pray for others? Did he pray primarily for himself and his mission?

THREE ANCIENT TEXTS

"Father,
hallowed be your name,
your kingdom come.
Give us each day our daily bread.
Forgive us our sins,
for we also forgive everyone who sins against us.
And lead us not into temptation."
THE GOSPEL ACCORDING TO LUKE
chapter 11 verses 2–4

"Our Father in heaven,
hallowed be your name,
your kingdom come,
your will be done,
on earth as it is in heaven.
Give us today our daily bread.
And forgive us our debts,
as we also have forgiven our debtors.
And lead us not into temptation,
but deliver us from the evil one.'
THE GOSPEL ACCORDING TO MATTHEW
chapter 6 verses 9–13

Our Father which art in heaven,
Hallowed be Thy name,
Thy kingdom come, Thy will be done,
as in heaven, so on earth;
Give us today our daily bread,
and forgive us our debt,
as we also forgive our debtors,
and lead us not into temptation,
but deliver us from evil;
for Thine is the power and the glory forever.
THE DIDACHE OF THE TWELVE APOSTLES
chapter 8

"Lord, teach us to pray,
just as John taught his disciples."
THE GOSPEL ACCORDING TO LUKE
Chapter 11 verse 1

I

A Teachable Moment

Jesus knew it was an opportune teachable moment when one of the disciples said, *"Lord, teach us to pray."* Good teachers live for teachable moments when their students are eager to learn, and Jesus was the consummate teacher who saw every common day occurrence—from birds in the air, to flowers in the field, to seeds wastefully spread on the hard ground—as potential teachable moments. Even Jesus' enemies conferred upon him the respected title of Rabbi; Good Teacher.

Teachable moments remind me of the popular 1970s television sitcom *Welcome Back Kotter* which was an unexpected success. Gabe Kotter, the main character, was a civics teacher of never-do-well remedial students in the Brooklyn, New York, high school where he himself had graduated. Mr. Kotter was constantly looking for teachable moments with his borderline at-risk students who adopted the self-deprecating nickname—*The Sweat Hogs.*

The most well-known Sweat Hog was the Italian wise guy, Vinnie Barbarino, played by future star, John Travolta. Then there was "Boom Boom" Washington, the tall African-American basketball player with athletic skills we viewers never saw in action. Juan Epstein was the diminutive Puerto Rican who repeatedly threatened to pull a switch-blade knife hidden on his body. It was a knife that he never once produced in all the seasons of this enormously successful television sitcom.

The most loveable character was Arnold Horshack, the insecure, out of place Jewish kid who struggled to fit in with the tougher, cooler guys. Mr. Kotter was continually looking for teachable moments with his Sweat Hogs and, when one occurred, insecure Arnold Horshack would throw his arm in the air and yell at the top of his voice: *"Oh, oh, oh ... call on me, Mr. Kotter, call on me!"*

When one of the disciples asked Jesus: *"LORD, teach us to pray,"* a teachable moment had arrived. It arrived because the disciples first observed that Jesus, the Supreme Example, went every day to *"a certain place"* to pray. At least one of the disciples felt that their band of brothers needed help with prayer.

New Testament scholar William Barclay sheds some extra light on this incident. He explained that it was the regular custom of a rabbi to teach his disciples a simple prayer which could be used daily as part of their group identity. Apparently John the Baptist had done this, and several of Jesus' disciples had been followers of John. In response to this teachable moment, Jesus taught his disciples what we commonly refer to as The LORD's Prayer.

Let's assume for a moment that we are in a teachable moment about the New Testament and how The LORD's Prayer has come to us.

We have three ancient sources for the words of this prayer that we repeat so often. The briefest form is found in the Gospel According to Luke. A slightly longer version is found in the Gospel According to Matthew. But the form closest to what Protestant Christians repeat is taken from an ancient treatise known as *"The Didache"* or *"The*

Teaching of the Twelve Apostles." This late first- or early second-century document was similar to a New Believers' Manual.

Luke, author of the briefest version of the prayer, was not an eyewitness to the life of Jesus. He was a second-generation Christian and the traveling companion of the apostle Paul. In the prologue to Luke's Gospel, he describes himself as an investigative reporter who sought out eyewitnesses in order to write an *"orderly account"* of *"the things that happened."*

One of the most highly regarded New Testament scholars regarding The LORD's Prayer in the last century was German Lutheran Professor Joachim Jeremias. He built a very convincing argument that Luke's briefer version of the prayer is the earliest and most accurate as to the original length and the actual words of Jesus.

Matthew's lengthier version reflects a more Jewish revision of Jesus' original words, frequently using the common rabbinic technique of parallelism, double-stating a concept to expand and clarify its meaning. The technique of parallelism is easy to identify in our English language versions of The LORD's Prayer:

Luke's Gospel simply says: *"Father, hallowed be your name."*

Matthew expands: *"Our Father in heaven, hallowed be your name."*

Luke says simply, *"Your kingdom come."*

Matthew adds, *"Your will be done,"* then explains *"on earth as it is in heaven."*

Luke says, *"Lead us not into temptation."*

Matthew further adds, *"but deliver us from evil."*

Both Luke and Matthew end abruptly. Only the early second-century version of the prayer found in *The Didache*, written decades after the Gospels, adds the final words which Protestants include but

Catholics exclude: *"For Yours is the kingdom, and the power, and the glory forever."*

The Didache refers to this prayer of Jesus, not as The LORD's Prayer, but as The Disciple's Prayer. These sacred words were only given to new followers of Jesus following baptism and participation in The LORD's Supper along with the instructions to *"pray these words three times daily."*

According to Professor Jeremias, the most revolutionary concept in this teachable moment is the very first phrase, *"Our Father."* God's name was so holy to the ancient Hebrews and to the Jews of Jesus' day that it could not be pronounced or even written. Shockingly, Jesus says we may address the unspeakably holy Creator God as *"Abba, Father."*

Jesus is saying in this profound teachable moment that we not only have permission, we have the highest conceivable invitation and encouragement to address the God whose name is unspeakable as *"Abba Father"!* We might even say, "Daddy!" Make no mistake, this was revolutionary!

Jesus was not giving his disciples a new name for God. This was a teachable moment about *relationship* with the Creator God. We are invited to assume a familial relationship with the God who is so totally *"other"* that His name is unspeakable.

The apostle Paul grasped this revolutionary concept and reminds us: *"For you did not receive a spirit that makes you a slave again to fear, but you received the Spirit of sonship. And by him we cry, 'Abba, Father.'"* (Romans 8:15–16 NIV) Paul is pointing to the familial relationship with God which Jesus alone taught.

Professor Jeremias concludes after a lengthy theological discourse that there is no parallel in the whole of Jewish literature prior to Jesus for this descriptive Aramaic word *"Abba"* in addressing God. We are confronted in this teachable moment with a revolutionary new way of thinking about our relationship with God.

In this teachable moment, Jesus' prayer is teaching us to want what God wants: the reign of His Kingdom to come on earth, and His Will to be done on earth, even as it is in heaven. If anyone takes this teachable moment seriously, then it is incumbent on followers of Jesus to join God's agenda.

Seriously consider: Is there anything you might want, or treasure, or expect, or even demand here on earth that God would never have in heaven? That ought to be a sobering question. As followers of Jesus, we should never pray for or advocate for anything on earth that God would not have in heaven. That is, if we take seriously this prayer that we repeat so casually so often.

> "As followers of Jesus, we should never pray for or advocate for anything on earth that God would not have in heaven."

Be careful, then, when you pray this revolutionary prayer Jesus taught his disciples. If God's Kingdom and God's Will should actually come on this earth, if God's Reign should actually take control of your life, it may not be what you think or expect.

This simple, easy-to-remember prayer that we Christians repeat so casually as part of our worship takes us back to the very words of Jesus himself. These words connect us with the first disciples who passed them on to the earliest followers of Jesus. This prayer connects us to all the believers from the time of Jesus to this very teachable moment we find ourselves in today.

This prayer repeated every week in worship connects us with all believers in the world today as they repeat the same words in virtually every language. These words bind together all ethnicities, languages, and cultures in the Kingdom of God on earth—even as it is in heaven. Additionally, there is nothing in this prayer that Jews or Muslims cannot pray with good conscience. This prayer can unite all people.

Maybe, just maybe, we are all remedial students in need of a teachable moment. Maybe we are all just Sweat Hogs in the School of Jesus. Some of us exhibit the same false bravado of Vinnie Barbarino's lack of self-esteem and self-worth. Maybe some walk with the same exaggerated swagger of "Boom Boom" Washington's modest athletic ability. Perhaps we wrap ourselves in the false assurance of some weapon of self-defense like Juan Epstein's never-revealed switchblade knife. Or maybe we are all like the overcompensating, insecure, approval-desperate Arnold Horshack—"Oww, oww, oww ... call on me, Jesus, call on me ... I know the answer!"

Perhaps Jesus has something revolutionary to teach us: more than just a model prayer, but about the very nature of God and our relationship to God as Our Father, and about what privilege we have in approaching God as citizens of His Kingdom.

Maybe, just maybe, we are in "A TEACHABLE MOMENT"!

For Personal Reflection or Group Interaction

Do you recall some special teachable moments in your life when your readiness to learn was especially evident?

How do you reconcile differences in the way the Gospels report the words and events in Jesus' life story, such as the wording of Our LORD's Prayer?

Is there anything you might want, or treasure, or expect, or even demand to have here on earth that God would not want in heaven?

Very early in the morning,
while it was still dark,
Jesus got up, left the house
and went off to a solitary place,
where he prayed.
THE GOSPEL ACCORDING TO MARK
chapter 1 verse 35

"But when you pray,
go into your room, close the door
and pray to your Father, who is unseen.
Then your Father,
who sees what is done in secret,
will reward you.
And when you pray,
do not keep on babbling like pagans,
for they think they will be heard
because of their many words.
Do not be like them,
for your Father knows what you need
before you ask him."
THE GOSPEL ACCORDING TO MATTHEW
chapter 6 verses 6–8
(from The Sermon on the Mount)

One day Jesus was praying
in a certain place...
THE GOSPEL ACCORDING TO LUKE
chapter 11 verse 1

A Certain Place

T he telephone has been used to illustrate prayer many times. Since cell phones and smart phones have come into existence, the illustration works even better because cell phones go with us wherever we are.

Some may automatically and erroneously think of prayer as similar to the autodial button to be used at any time in any place to quickly dial God's number. That is not a good, healthy, or even accurate picture of prayer or our relationship to God. The Creator God is not at our disposal to call at some whim whenever we need help. We do not beckon the Creator God!

The more accurate picture of prayer is the cell phone is constantly ringing and God is at the other end of the line calling all the time. The only question is—will you answer God's call? Prayer is our response to God's initiative. God is continually in the initiative, reaching out to us. And all too often, we simply ignore God and fail to answer.

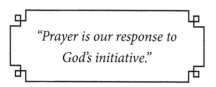

"*Prayer is our response to God's initiative.*"

The example of Jesus is that he set aside a certain time early in the day to go to a "certain place" to be alone with God in prayer—to deliberately respond to God's call. The Garden of Gethsemane may very well have been one of those "certain places" to which Jesus returned on multiple occasions. Perhaps it is the place where Jesus met Nicodemus the Pharisee at night because Nicodemus was reluctant to be seen with Jesus in the light of day.

Marcus Borg describes how ancient Celtic Christians of Ireland and Scotland believed in what they called *"thin places."* Thin places were where the reality of this earthly life and the reality of the kingdom of heaven would intersect and meet. The Celtic people believed that there were certain places and times when the Creator God who is transcendent—*so much more* than right here, right now—is experienced as immanent—*right here, right now.*

Thin places are those times and places when we actually experience the sacred presence of God. If we establish that "certain place" and "certain time" to spend alone with God, to deliberately answer God's call on the cell phone of life, it can become a time and place to look forward to; certainly not a burden to dread or avoid.

If we cultivate that certain time and certain place, conversation with God will become more natural. We are far more likely to learn how to *"pray without ceasing"*—as the apostle Paul admonished, and as Jesus most certainly did—if we first learn to pray faithfully in a certain place at a certain time.

There have been many certain times and places in my life, some *"thinner"* than others. Those places and times became *"thin places"* because that was when and where I made myself available to be aware of God's Presence. Those places and times have shifted through the years, but they have always required cultivation. They do not happen without special effort.

Some time ago, in response to my cardiologist who in a tactful but unmistakable way said that I was overweight and lazy, I decided to cultivate a new *"thin place"* (no pun intended). I wanted to accomplish several things with one activity.

Early in the morning, rather than sitting in my favorite *"thin place"*—which was my cushy chair with ottoman—I would ride my bicycle out to the lighthouse on the peninsula in the lake community where I'm fortunate to live.

At that location, early in the morning, I expected to experience the beautiful sunrise and commune with God in the beauty of God's Creation with the water lapping the shore on either side of the peninsula before the day got too hot.

In the beginning, this was not a *"thin place"* experience. It was a *"thick place"* experience. Thick with humidity, trembling legs, shortness of breath, near exhaustion, and soaking perspiration. But over time it became *"thinner and thinner,"* until it really became one of the most memorable and meaningful *"thin places"* I ever expect to enjoy.

Personally, I do not find prayer or cultivating a *"thin place"* to be easy, and I suspect that is a pretty universal phenomenon. Quaker theologian and mystic, Richard Foster, has written that

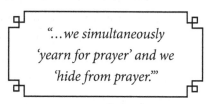

"...we simultaneously 'yearn for prayer' and we 'hide from prayer.'"

we simultaneously "yearn for prayer" while at the same time, we "hide from prayer." Foster writes with great empathy for those who find prayer to be difficult. He suggests beginning your prayers with total honesty: "God, I don't want to pray, but I want to want to pray." Honesty in prayer is essential. Who do we think we are fooling?

Dietrich Bonhoeffer, the famous German pastor, theologian, and martyr in World War II, was noted by his fellow concentration camp prisoners for both the habit and the intensity of his daily prayers. Even as spiritual a man as Bonhoeffer said: "Although prayer is the expression of a universal human instinct, it is by no means an obvious or natural activity."

We all come to the practice of prayer with different emotional and spiritual assets and liabilities which we received from our unique life experiences. For some people those life experiences are helpful and beneficial. For others, their life experiences are detrimental to trusting and seeking God. We all come from very different backgrounds. We don't need to be judgmental about the level of difficulty or ease anyone experiences in cultivating a certain place and certain time for prayer. Yet, we all have the same need to pray regardless of the difficulty or ease.

How does one cultivate a certain time and place that can potentially become a "thin place"? There is no shortcut or end run around a deliberate decision. You must make a commitment. Chose the place. Set the time. Then make that time and place a priority.

Lots of words in prayer are not necessary for everyone, and sometimes not helpful. Good posture is helpful. Silence is golden. Mental pictures have been helpful to me. Picture in your mind anyone you are concerned about. Picture what he or she looks like in the dilemma or need that causes the concern you feel for them.

An example: our church lost the most incredible, capable, and magnificent pianist and organist imaginable. The likelihood of our small community finding another musician of the same quality was slim to none. I didn't need words to express my concern or my uneasiness over the prospect of a worship experience diminished by less than excellent musicianship. My prayer was simply a mental picture of the empty piano bench in front of our sanctuary's baby grand piano. Words were unnecessary and carried far less emotional meaning than that mental picture of an empty piano bench. Eventually the empty piano bench was occupied by a new capable person.

It's amazing how many pictures come to mind. Far more meaningful and effective for me than beginning with words. Sometimes the mental pictures are of an incident from the past. The mental picture arrives unwanted and unexpected. It may be something I deeply regret. That is, I believe, the Spirit bringing to my mind something that still requires confession and repentance until I have finally forgiven myself even as God has forgiven me.

Sometimes the mental image is one that causes feelings of gratitude and thankfulness. Other times it is a signal to be concerned about a particular person or situation. Then the words of prayer, which for whatever reason are the hardest part for me, the words of prayer attached to that mental picture come naturally without effort or forethought.

After years of struggling with prayer programs and prayer lists and feelings of being an unspiritual failure, this form of restful quietness, at a certain time and certain place, have finally become not a boring routine but an anticipated time of contemplation and a quiet place of peace without pressure to perform.

The priority Jesus placed on a certain time and a certain place have proven true for me. A certain time in a certain place have repeatedly become "thin places." It is, in my experience, the best way to begin.

Years ago, before I got wiser (assuming I have ever gotten any wiser), I was hoodwinked into helping move an elderly lady from her home into an assisted living facility. It was against her will, but everyone involved felt it was necessary.

She had outlived all her family and had few friends left. Those to whom she had given power of attorney were rightfully concerned that she be in a safe circumstance. They requested her pastor's help—so that she could be angry with me as well as them. That was my lack of wisdom. It would have been much wiser if she only harbored anger toward them and not me as her pastor also.

She was a retired librarian. Librarians of her generation were not people to be messed with! All of us were afraid of her wrath that day. When it became apparent that she was not going to intimidate any of us into changing the plan, she took up residence in her favorite Queen Anne armchair next to her favorite lamp table where she kept her Bible. She moved the Bible from the table to her lap, and said with tears in her eyes: "Please bring my chair and lamp. It's where I meet the LORD every morning."

That was her highest priority and what she valued most at that point in her life, and it made perfect sense. It really doesn't take much to create a "*thin place*" in this world. A chair and a table with a lamp will do.

It can become "**a certain place.**"

For Personal Reflection or Group Interaction

What is your personal history of memorable "certain places" where you had meaningful times with God?

What techniques or helps do you utilize in your prayer life, such as lists, or patterns?

Is there a difference between your audible public prayer and your private inaudible inner prayer? Should there be a difference?

To what do you attribute the difficulty or ease you experience in establishing a certain time and place for prayer?

Then he said to them,
"Suppose you have a friend,
and you go to him at midnight and say,
`Friend, lend me three loaves of bread,
a friend of mine on a journey has come to me,
and I have no food to offer him.'
And suppose the one inside answers,
`Don't bother me. The door is already locked,
and my children and I are already in bed.
I can't get up and give you anything.'
I tell you, even though he will not get up and give you the bread
because of friendship, yet because of your shameless audacity
he will surely get up and give you as much as you need.

"So I say to you:
Ask and it will be given to you;
seek and you will find;
knock and the door will be opened to you.
For everyone who asks receives;
the one who seeks finds;
and to him who knocks,
the door will be opened.

Which of you fathers,
if your son asks for a fish,
will give him a snake instead?
Or if he asks for an egg, will give him a scorpion?
If you then, though you are evil,
know how to give good gifts to your children,
how much more will your Father in heaven
give the Holy Spirit to those who ask him!"
THE GOSPEL ACCORDING TO LUKE
chapter 11 verses 5–13

III

WHAT GOD IS NOT LIKE

H ave you ever dealt with a salesman who just would not take NO for an answer? There is nothing more infuriating than such an inconsiderate and insensitive person who just doesn't get it. It brings out the worst in everyone involved.

Jesus immediately followed the profound "teachable moment"— where he shared his brief model prayer—with a parable about just such a person. The determined nighttime borrower knocked with shame-less audacity and persistence. That is what the Greek word in the text means. He shamelessly persisted in knocking until at last the sleeping neighbor, knowing that the whole family was awakened anyway, got up and gave the obnoxious unrelenting neighbor what he wanted.

A parable is a story that is "laid alongside a truth" in order to better explain or illustrate that truth. Parables of Jesus typically tell us a truth about the nature of God, or the Kingdom of God, or what it means to be a citizen living under God's reign.

What point is Jesus making in this parable? Is he telling us some-thing about how to shamelessly persist in prayer? Or is Jesus telling

19

us something about the nature of God in response to prayer? Is the lesson of this parable that we should be like the obnoxious neighbor, persistent in prayer until God reluctantly gives in to our demands? Must we pound at God's door until we finally compel God—out of weariness—to get up and give us what we desire or need? Must we shamelessly persist in prayer until we have coerced an unwilling God to act on our behalf?

One does not live in the Christian life and church community for very long before discovering that there are numerous viewpoints regarding prayer. On one extreme there are those who say: What difference does prayer make? Everything is going to happen as it happens. Life is what it is. It's all pre-determined. If your prayer is answered like you want, it was going to happen anyway. It's just coincidence. Prayer may make you feel better, but it doesn't change anything.

A closely related more moderate viewpoint: Prayer is learning to pray in agreement with God's Will so that you pray for what God intended all along. Agreement with God's Will in prayer only comes through wisdom and persistent practice over time

On the other extreme are those who believe: If God is God, then He *can* do and *will* do anything if you just pray long enough and hard enough and with faith enough. There are innumerable stopping points on the continuum between these two extremes.

In order to rightly understand the lesson of this parable, we must first grasp the most revolutionary concept in Our LORD's Prayer, the very first word: *Abba, Father.* As has been stated earlier: this was not Jesus giving God a new name. It announced the relationship we have with God. Jesus was saying to his disciples, and thus to us, we are talking with our heavenly Dad; *Abba Father.*

Whatever else this parable may be teaching, it must be consistent with this radically important Truth about the relationship Jesus says we have with God. If a parable is a story "laid alongside of a Truth" in order to make that Truth more plain to understand, then there is one explanation of this parable that is consistent with *Abba Father*. William Barclay says it is a parable of contrast. It teaches us what God is like by illustrating what God is not like.

Abba Father is not like a reluctant, disgruntled neighbor getting up in the middle of the night out of some sense of obligation. Jesus then drives home his point about our child-parent relationship with God: *If we imperfect parents know how to give good gifts to our children, how much more does our Father in heaven give good gifts to His children who ask Him?*

This parable teaches us what kind of permission, even encouragement, we have in making our petitions to God in prayer. We, like the neighbor who came in the middle of the night, are encouraged to ask God boldly without hesitation or reluctance, even with shameless persistence. But be assured: God is **not** like that reluctant neighbor.

The whole subject of prayer is a bottomless barrel of emotional, spiritual, and intellectual issues, mystery, and even contradictions, not the least of which is those shamelessly persistent prayers which seem to be appropriate in relation to God's Kingdom values but also seem to go unanswered.

If God is God, especially *Abba Father*, then there is no such thing as an unanswered prayer. Perhaps the Big Truth of this parable is: Prayer is *not* primarily about getting what we ask for. Prayer *is*

> "*Prayer is about receiving what we most need. What we most need is a relationship with Abba Father.*"

about receiving what we most need. What we most need is a relationship with *Abba Father*.

This unusual parable of Jesus concludes with what we will always receive when we ask, seek, and knock with or without shameless persistence: *"How much more will your Father in heaven give the Holy Spirit to those who ask him."*

The Truth of this parable may be illustrated by this apocryphal prayer reportedly found on the body of an anonymous Confederate soldier:

I asked God for strength that I might achieve.
I was made weak that I might learn humbly to obey.

I asked God for health that I might do greater things.
I was given infirmity that I might do better things.

I asked God for riches that I might be happy.
I was given poverty that I might be wise.

I asked God for power that I might have the praise of men.
I was given weakness that I might feel the need of God.

I asked God for all things that I might enjoy life.
I was given life that I might enjoy all things.

I got nothing that I asked for, but everything I hoped for.
Almost despite myself, my unspoken prayers were answered.

I am, among all men, most richly blessed.

When Jesus returned from praying in his "certain place" and encountered this unique "teachable moment" with his disciples, he concluded the prayer that he taught them with this parable to illustrate and drive home the Truth that He was teaching. Prayer is not about getting what you ask for nearly so much as it is about cultivating what you most need—a relationship with Abba Father.

In this Parable, unique to Luke's Gospel and found nowhere else, we learn what God is like by learning WHAT GOD IS NOT LIKE. The Truth from this parable is a most profound teachable moment.

For Personal Reflection or Group Interaction

How do you feel about the results of prayer? What is the effect of prayer in your life?

How do you balance persistence in prayer with prayers that appear to be unanswered?

How do you respond to the perspective that prayer is primarily about relationship with God rather than getting what you pray for?

He said to them, "When you pray, say:
Father, hallowed be your name...
THE GOSPEL ACCORDING TO LUKE
chapter 11 verse 2

This, then, is how you should pray:
"'Our Father in heaven."
THE GOSPEL ACCORDING TO MATTHEW
chapter 6 verse 9
(The Sermon on the Mount)

"But while he was still a long way off,
his father saw him and
was filled with compassion for him;
he ran to his son,
threw his arms around him
and kissed him.
THE GOSPEL ACCORDING TO LUKE
chapter 15 verse 20
(The Parable of the Prodigal Son)

IV

OUR FATHER

P ersonally, I have no memory of being taught The LORD's Prayer. In fact, I have no memory of not already knowing The LORD's Prayer. That's how thorough my Christian family upbringing was. But I do have memories and experiences of how impactful this short prayer can be.

For several months I was a chaplain at the Baptist Medical Center Hospital in downtown San Antonio. The chaplains would joke among ourselves about the "Baptist Hospital for Catholics" because so many of the families we served in downtown San Antonio were Catholic. One of the many wonderful things I learned in that experience was the strong religious bonding in Mexican-American Catholic families.

Catholic believers commonly refer to The LORD's Prayer as the *"Our Father."* As a Protestant chaplain to Catholic families in times of crisis, one of the most effective ways I found to build connection and rapport was to simply pray the *"Our Father"* together with them. It was plain to see how comforting and reassuring these familiar words could be. It was also obvious how much reverence and sincerity Catholic families brought to these familiar words repeated so frequently.

Another place where these familiar words took on special significance was at the conclusion of AA Meetings. I am not a participant in Alcoholics Anonymous, but it has been my great privilege to be included in AA meetings as an outsider on rare occasions. For those alcohol- or drug-addicted persons who have "found bottom," these familiar words take on significant meaning that the rest of us, who feel like we are "on top" of life, never quite experience.

The AA meetings that I attended most often were at a halfway house for women recovering from addiction. I sometimes led their Bible study. These women were from all walks of life. The diversity was shocking: affluent older women, young suburban housewives and mothers, professional working women, down and out street-walking prostitutes, women recently incarcerated. But a frequent common denominator among women with addiction—no matter what their background—was a tragic history with their earthly fathers. Physical violence and sexual abuse were not uncommon.

My role as the non-addicted male person in their midst was to talk about what God is really like, in place of whatever negative life experience many may have acquired. The very first words of Our LORD's Prayer could be, for some of these women, an almost insurmountable emotional wall to climb. Father or Dad or Daddy was not a word that carried positive memories for many of these women.

One way of looking at the life and teaching of Jesus is this: Jesus came to correct all the wrong notions and ideas that the world has accumulated about God, or that negative life experiences may have taught us.

Even though technically speaking God is spirit and without gender, we inevitably use human imagery and language to speak of God. All language about God is by necessity some kind of metaphorical analogy. It is unavoidable and inevitable that we speak of God in human analogies.

The primary human analogy that Jesus used to describe God was *"Abba, Father."* Over 150 times in the Gospel accounts Jesus refers to God as *Abba* Father. Although fewer and less well known, there are female and maternal characteristics of God also found in the scriptures. Yet Fatherhood is apparently the most powerful, and certainly the most frequent descriptive metaphor for God in the New Testament. The Fatherhood of God must accurately describe how God relates to us and how we can respond as children. In the paternalistic culture in which Jesus lived, it was the most natural metaphor for him to use. But the emphasis of the metaphor is not the maleness of God but the familial parental relationship God desires to have with us.

Unfortunately, none of us had perfect parents. None of us have been perfect parents. Everyone without exception carries emotional baggage from both parenting and being parented. With that in mind, I ran a small-scale experiment with several of my preacher buddies several years ago. I used an approach I learned from one of my hospital chaplain supervisors.

I posed this question with the promise to reciprocate if my pastor friend would participate: *Give yourself 20 seconds to think, then tell me your earliest memory of your father.* It really didn't matter if it was actually their earliest memory. What mattered was the first memory that came to mind. Then we explored the implications of that memory to their relationship with God. In most cases, it was revealing in some significant way that "rang true" to each of their lives.

Some of the more memorable responses from these pastor friends:

First childhood memory: Dad walking through the house throwing off light switches and complaining about wasting electricity.

Life Implication: A scarcity mentality. God is stingy and tight with resources and at least a little angry. There is not enough to go around. My pastor friend was continually concerned about running out of money or resources, he struggled with faith in God's provision, and was so financially conservative it sometimes affected his family. He also became a more reflective role model for others. He could hear his own drumbeat above the noise of popular culture.

First childhood memory: Swimming with Dad in water over his head; he reached out for Dad who pushed him away with the order, "Keep swimming."

Life Implication: Swim or sink; no one will rescue you. You must depend on yourself, not God. There's no point in praying, it all depends on you. The connection between this memory and his difficulty praying "rang true" to him. But he has also become a self-reliant and reliable pastor and shepherd loved by many.

First childhood memory: Fishing at night on the gulf coast with his dad, he was afraid to step out of the lantern light into the dark to get the tackle box. As his dad stomped past him to get the tackle box, he said, "Sissy!" That memory stuck!

Life Implication: Always had to prove his courage no matter what. God demands courageous action. God is angry at weakness. Proving his courage has tended to get him in trouble throughout his life. He has also become a dynamic leader and catalyst for change.

First childhood memory: Looking at an animal picture book during nap time, he was unaware that his dad was looking over his shoulder. He said out loud to himself: "I wonder what that is?" Dad surprised him from behind and said: "It's a hippopotamus."

Life Implication: God is an ever-present reality, always watching over him to help in times of need. He became an encouraging kind of pastor whose prayer life reflected that comforting knowledge of God's presence. His self-assurance of God's leadership often pulled him out in front of where his congregation was willing to follow; an ironic outcome.

We all carry memories of parents and parenting—some helpful, some painful—that subconsciously impact our disposition toward trusting God our Heavenly Father and our faith development. I shudder to think how my own children would answer that same question and what life implications my actions might have had for them.

This approach is based in the life cycle faith development theory of James W. Fowler. Fowler differentiates faith from both belief and religion. From this perspective, faith is an emotional dimension of personal development apart from cognitive content or religious tradition. Every person leaves childhood and adolescence with a different set of assets or liabilities in personal capacity for faith. In this developmental theory, an atheistic or agnostic person may have greater faith capacity than a religious person who believes in God. Conversely, a very religious person may struggle with faith.

> *"Every person has a different set of assets or liabilities in personal capacity for faith."*

All the more reason it is critically important to understand as much as possible about what Jesus meant when He said God is *"Our Father."* The most graphic story Jesus told about the Fatherhood of God is most often referred to as "The Story of the Prodigal Son" when in fact, it should be called "The Story of the Loving Father."

It is not necessarily a good story about parenting as such. It is certainly not a good story about how to distribute one's wealth as inheritance. But it is Jesus' most graphic story about the character and nature of God as Our Father.

Perhaps we all have a mental picture of the Loving Father in this story, but this is my picture: An elderly man goes out on his front porch every morning to enjoy his coffee and read the newspaper. He leans over the porch railing and looks down the road to his left, but sees nothing of interest on the dusty road. He settles into his rocking chair and unfolds the newspaper to read the day's news as he does every day.

Periodically he lowers the paper and glances off to the left, down the road, but returns to his paper. Finally he folds the paper, gets up, and goes to the rail for one last look before going inside. The day is warming up, and it's getting humid.

Off in the distance he sees a figure coming up the road. He lowers his glasses to focus a little better. There is something familiar in that walk. The old man carefully walks down the porch steps holding onto the rail, then walks quickly out to the sidewalk while still looking off to the left. He reaches the picket fence, goes through the gate, and turns left onto the dusty road. He breaks into a run in an old man's awkward gait.

The figure in the road has stopped with his head hung low as the old man reaches him in a huge bear hug embrace. Nothing in the past matters. All is forgiven. That wasted boy, that drug addicted girl, that shamed prodigal child is YOU. It's me. It's all of us. Our Heavenly Father will always welcome us home no matter what we have done. That is the graphic picture of what Jesus means by *Abba Father*.

Since God is *Our Father*, we all have a common parentage. God is not just *MY* Father, or *YOUR* Father: He is *OUR* Father. We are all brothers and sisters regardless of our human parentage, culture, nationality, ethnicity, or any other factor. We share a common Creator, the One and only True God.

One of my favorite quotes which I heard my longtime mentor, Buckner Fanning, use many times is attributed to British novelist and journalist of the nineteenth century, G. K. Chesterton: *"We are all in a leaky boat on a stormy sea and we owe one another a terrible loyalty."* We are brothers and sisters in Christ.

Based upon Jesus' description of God as *Our Father*, He must want only what is good and best for each of us. He would never desire our harm. He knows more about our needs than we do. In fact, He knows what we need before we ask. Therefore, He invites our requests: an acknowledgement of His love and our dependence on Him.

Since God is *Our Father*, we need not be reluctant in speaking our minds or sharing our heart's true desires. God desires our honesty. We may, by our actions, add stress to our fellowship with a loving parent, but nothing can ever break or change the parent-child relationship. God never ceases to be *Our Father*.

Like all good parents, He loves us more than we love ourselves. Another favorite quote I first learned from Buckner, this time attributed to St. Augustine: *"He loves each one of us as though there was but one of us to love."* What a thought!

Most important of all, since God is *Our Father*, sin and forgiveness take on an entirely new meaning. Our sins are not against some sterile code of conduct, system of justice, or impersonal law. Our sins are not against a stern judge who desires to pronounce

> *"Our sins are against a loving Father whose greatest desire is to forgive and restore."*

punishment. Our sins are against a loving Father whose greatest desire is to forgive and restore. He is always looking for our return.

Since God is *Our Father*, our lives are forever changed and made different. That is the critically all-important teachable moment that Jesus came to give us. The tragedy is what happens when unhealthy religion replaces this all-important picture of God as *Abba Father* with judgmental exclusive legalism. The true story of Alexander Hamilton is such an example.

Hamilton was an extraordinary model of entrepreneurial ingenuity and industry from a young age. He excelled and succeeded against almost insurmountable odds to become George Washington's strong right-hand man during and after the Revolutionary War. An author of the Federalist Papers, he was also the military strategist who launched the US Navy. As the first secretary of the Treasury, he was the financial genius who created Wall Street.

In the opening pages of William Sterne Randall's biography, Hamilton lay mortally wounded following a duel with Aaron Burr, vice president of the United States under President Thomas Jefferson. According to witnesses, Hamilton made clear both before and after the duel that he had no intention of firing at Burr.

Hamilton realized instantly that he had received a mortal wound. The ball entered his left side and lodged in his vertebrae, severing his spine and paralyzing his legs. He was moved to a nearby farmhouse where he called for his wife and children and asked for a minister of the Gospel.

The first minister summoned was the Episcopal bishop of New York. It was well known that Hamilton faithfully led and maintained Episcopal prayers with his family in their home. They observed Matins every morning and Vespers every evening, although he had not attended church services since the end of the Revolutionary War.

The bishop refused Hamilton's request for Communion for two reasons. As the illegitimate bastard child of a mistress, Hamilton had never been baptized. In fact, he was refused baptism more than once due to the sins of his mother. Unbaptized, he had never been allowed to receive Communion. The bishop did not want to set the precedent of offering communion to the unbaptized. Secondly, the bishop did not want to appear to condone dueling.

Hamilton then sent for the pastor of the church where he had undergone a conversion experience as a twelve-year-old bastard orphan. He had been refused baptism and communion at that time because the pastor did not want to condone the lifestyle of his deceased mother as the mistress of a married man.

The current pastor responded to the summons. Upon arrival he informed Hamilton that he could only receive baptism and communion in the church, at the altar, during a regular Sunday worship service.

It had been 24 hours since Hamilton was wounded and he was fading steadily. The bishop of New York was called again. The bishop confessed his desire to "help a fellow mortal in distress" but he must "unequivocally condemn dueling" and not offer communion to a participant in that "barbaric custom."

According to the physician at the bedside, Hamilton agreed with him "in sorrow and contrition." Upon that confession, the bishop exacted from Hamilton a vow that—if he should survive—he would never duel again and would use his influence to oppose the practice. This was a promise Hamilton found easy to make.

The bishop required a pledge that he would "live in love and charity with all men and bore no ill will to Aaron Burr."

Hamilton pledged, "I forgive all that has happened."

Writhing in agony, Hamilton received his first communion "with great devotion" and according to the physician, "his heart appeared to be perfectly at rest." On July 12, 1804, shortly after noon, following 31 hours of agony, with the bishop of New York at his bedside, Alexander Hamilton died at age forty-nine.

Now, consider the response of the Father in Jesus' parable about the Prodigal Son: *"But while he was still a long way off, his father saw him and was filled with compassion for him; he ran to his son, threw his arms around him and kissed him."*

How can these two stories be reconciled with each other? Is there any way to calculate how much damage has been done to the Good News of Jesus Christ in the name of self-righteous legalistic religion? The fear of condoning sin? The fear of public opinion or of setting a precedent? Did Jesus not set the precedent we should follow a long time ago in both word and example and in this parable about a loving father?

What does this model prayer which tells us that God is *OUR Father* and that we are citizens in His Kingdom—what does it mean? How should citizens of God's Kingdom behave toward one another in light of the brotherhood of all mankind and the Fatherhood of God taught by Jesus in only the first two words of this prayer?

This prayer is worth considering again and again. As often as we pray these two simple but revolutionary words:

"Our Father..."

For Personal Reflection or Group Interaction

How do you feel Alexander Hamilton should have been treated by the church as an illegitimate child of a mistress?

Do you find any justification for the actions of the bishop and the pastor?

Do we live with modern-day parallels to Hamilton's experience with the church? If so, what are they and what should we do differently? For instance, should we baptize the adopted children of homosexual couples?

Give yourself 20 seconds to think. What is your earliest memory of your earthly father? (It really doesn't matter if it is your earliest memory; what matters is the first memory that comes to mind. If you did not know your father, recall the person who was your primary parental figure.)

Explore with a trusted friend or group if there might be some meaningful connection between your remembered experience with your earthly father and your trust relationship with your Heavenly Father.

God said to Moses,
"I AM WHO I AM.
This is what you are to say to the Israelites:
'I AM has sent me to you.'
God also said to Moses,
"Say to the Israelites,
'The LORD, the God of your fathers
-the God of Abraham, the God of Isaac
and the God of Jacob-
has sent me to you.'
This is my name forever,
the name you shall call me
from generation to generation.
EXODUS
chapter 3 verses 14–15

"Father, hallowed be your name...."
THE GOSPEL ACCORDING TO LUKE
chapter 11 verse 2

"'Our Father in heaven,
hallowed be your name...."
THE GOSPEL ACCORDING TO MATTHEW
chapter 6 verse 9

Therefore God exalted him to the highest place
and gave him the name that is above every name,
that at the name of Jesus every knee should bow,
in heaven and on earth and under the earth,
and every tongue acknowledge that Jesus Christ is Lord,
to the glory of God the Father.
THE LETTER OF PAUL TO THE PHILIPPIANS
chapter 2 verses 9–11

V

HALLOWED NAME

What's in a name? Not much. Just your identity and reputation. That's all.

Nicknames can tell us something important about a person. For instance, several friends who have known me for a long time call me *IrReverend*. That is not exactly a high recommendation for a pastor, but thankfully it is used with tongue-in-cheek affection.

Grandparent names can tell us a lot. My brother's grandparent name is *Grumpy*. His wife's grandparent name is *Happy*. I quickly add *Grumpy* does not portray the truth about my brother's personality, especially with his grandchildren. Go figure.

God had a propensity for changing people's names to reflect who He desired them to become and what He planned to do through them. Abram's name was changed to Abraham which meant *"father of many nations."* Sarai was changed to Sarah which meant *"mother of many nations."* Jacob, whose name meant *deceiver*, lived down to his name, but he lived up to his new God-given name, Israel, which meant *"one who struggles with God."*

The most notable and memorable name change in the New Testament was Simon Peter. His original name was Simon which Jesus changed to *Cephas* in Aramaic. In the Greek language of the New Testament it was *Petros,* which along with *Cephas,* means *Rock* or *Stone.* We transliterate *Petros* in Greek to *Peter* in English. It is actually a more accurate translation to call him *Simon Rocky* than Simon Peter.

As a pastor, remembering names has been a full-time job. Over the years I have gotten so many names wrong it's been embarrassing. I've had entire conversations calling the other person by the wrong name. Many times, folks are too polite to correct me. Some are indignant. Once—but *only* once—I got the groom's name wrong in a wedding. That was definitely memorable.

When I was a college student, I worked at an insurance company. The founder and chairman of the board was an older gentleman who continually got my name wrong. He routinely called me Jim instead of John. I never felt that I should correct him. When I returned from active duty military service, I went to see him. My purpose was to request his reference as I was looking for a part-time job so that I could return to school. He greeted me as always in the past, "Jim, so glad to see you. How can I help you?"

As usual, I didn't correct him, but explained my mission to find a part-time job. He immediately swiveled in his chair, picked up the phone, and called the bank across the street where he served on the board of directors. As he explained my need of a job and that he was sending me over, I panicked, "He is about to give them the wrong name!" To my surprise, he said, "His name is John White and he will be there shortly." Then he hung up the phone and swiveled in his chair to face me. With a smile he said, "OK, Jim. It's all set. They are expecting you." Then he explained where to go and who to ask for.

To this day, nearly fifty years later, I'm still not sure if the name confusion was deliberate or some kind of test, but I knew it was important to report in with the correct name at the bank across the street. With his recommendation connected to the correct name, I landed a great part-time job for going back to school.

On those occasions through the years when my parents came to visit us, and I had opportunity to introduce my dad to friends, I would typically say, "This is my dad, JP White." In that brief introduction, you learned two important things: the relationship, my dad, and his preferred name, JP. The distinction is important.

In Our LORD's Prayer we are given permission, even encouragement, to address God as *"Our Father."* That is the familial relationship we are privileged to have with the Creator God. But in the very next phrase we are reminded that His Name is always to be treated with reverence. The name of God is so holy, so completely *other* than what we can know or understand, that we don't know what God's name really is beyond *I Am.*

In the Old Testament various words are used in reference to God, but they are not God's name. The word most often translated as God is *Elohim.* That is the word in Genesis 1 when it says: *"In the beginning God (Elohim) created...."* It is derived from the Middle Eastern Semitic word *"El"* which was used to refer to all gods, such as *Bael.*

But the word used for God's name, variously referred to as *Yahweh* or *Jehovah*, is in actuality unpronounceable. We are only guessing at its pronunciation because it is represented by four consonants without vowels: YHWH. In the Hebrew tradition, God's name is written in this unpronounceable consonant-form because it is unspeakable.

The reverence with which the Hebrew people treated the name of God is so great that it was never fully written, or ever spoken. Even modern-day Jewish writers in the English language will most often write *G-d*.

The word most often used to refer to God in the Old Testament is *Adonai*, which is translated LORD. Rather than a name, it is actually a title referring to the role God is to have in our lives. He is to be LORD over our lives.

So when we pray as Jesus taught us to pray: *"Our Father who art in heaven, hallowed be thy name..."*—we are invited and encouraged to address God in terms of our universal family relationship to God, *"Our Father."* Then immediately we are reminded of the unspeakable reverence with which we approach the unpronounceable name of the Creator God.

When we pray *"hallowed be thy name..."*—that God's unspeakable name should be reverenced in all the earth—we are praying that our own conduct should be a positive reflection of God's character, and that His reputation should be upheld by our conduct. Consider this line from the 23rd Psalm:

> *"...our conduct should be a positive reflection of God's character."*

"He leads me in paths of righteousness for His name's sake."

Our conduct reflects not just upon ourselves, but upon the character and reputation of the one who is LORD of our lives: the one we follow.

Perhaps the most remarkable turn of events in scriptural history is when the thoroughly monotheistic Jewish scholar, Saul of Tarsus, who learned from childhood how to reverence the unspeakable, never-written, unpronounceable name of the Most High God—quoted the first Christian hymn recorded in the New Testament: *"That at the name of Jesus every knee should bow, in heaven and on earth and under the earth, and every tongue confess that Jesus Christ is LORD, to the glory of God the Father."* Think about the significance of that!

So, what's in a name?

Not much. Just the whole of one's identity and reputation. That's all.

It is a teachable moment.

In the NAME of the Father, and the Son, and the Holy Spirit. Amen.

For Personal Reflection or Group Interaction

How do you typically address the Most High God in your personal and private prayers? Do you address God by name, by title, or by relationship? Do you address God differently in pubic audible prayer than you do in private silent prayer?

The second of the Ten Commandments says that we should not take the name of the LORD our God in vain. In light of the reverence God's name is due, what does that commandment mean to you in practice?

Jesus went into Galilee,
proclaiming the good news of God.
"The time has come," he said.
"The kingdom of God has come near.
Repent and believe the good news!"
THE GOSPEL ACCORDING TO MARK
chapter 1 verses14–15

"This, then, is how you should pray:
"'Our Father in heaven,
hallowed be your name,
your kingdom come...'"
THE GOSPEL ACCORDING TO MATTHEW
chapter 6 verse 9–10

Once, on being asked by the Pharisees
when the Kingdom of God would come,
Jesus replied, *"The coming of the kingdom of God*
is not something that can be observed,
nor will people say, 'Here it is,' or 'There it is,'
because the kingdom of God is in your midst."
THE GOSPEL ACCORDING TO LUKE
chapter 17 verses 20–21

Jesus said (to Pilate),
"My kingdom is not of this world.
If it were, my servants would fight
to prevent my arrest by the Jewish leaders.
But now my kingdom is from another place."
THE GOSPEL ACCORDING TO JOHN
chapter 18 verse 36

VI

THY KINGDOM COME

The Kingdom of God was the heart of Jesus' message. It was the focal point of Jesus' parables, telling us what life would be like if God is King and if we live under His reign. *"Thy Kingdom Come"* is also the central petition of The Lord's Prayer. Jesus instructs us to pray for God's Kingdom to come on earth even as it is already in heaven. Tellingly, the Kingdom of God and the Kingdom of Heaven are interchangeable in Jesus' parables.

Jesus had much to say about the Kingdom of God, and his ideas and concepts about the Kingdom were many and diverse. He is recorded speaking of the Kingdom of God forty-nine times in Matthew's Gospel, sixteen times in Mark's Gospel, and thirty-eight times in Luke's Gospel. The Kingdom of God is used over 150 times in the New Testament as a whole.

Since Jesus is recorded speaking most often about the Kingdom of God in Matthew's Gospel, we will take a survey of what it says there. Beginning in the Sermon on the Mount—Jesus proclaimed that the Kingdom was *for the poor in spirit*: those who are most discouraged and feel least deserving of God's favor. The Kingdom is also for those who feel *persecuted for righteousness*. From the world's point of view, neither of these conditions or circumstances is very desirable.

Nonetheless, the Kingdom is where to *store your treasure*, a place where it can never be destroyed, rust, decay, or go away. In fact, according to Jesus, if we seek God's Kingdom first, above all else, then all our other needs will already be met.

God's Kingdom may begin small as a mustard seed, but it will grow into a mighty tree. Like yeast in bread dough, it invisibly permeates; it is invasive and pervasive.

There is no scarcity, but there is abundance in God's Kingdom. It is like seed scattered so lavishly on both good soil and bad soil that it is wasteful. Like a treasure hidden in a field, or a rare pearl of enormous value, the Kingdom is worth whatever it takes to lay hold of it. Sell everything you have, if you must, to lay hold of it.

No one is undesirable in God's Kingdom. It is like a net let down into the sea to make a great catch of fish: as many as possible are wanted, all sizes and all types.

Unlike the way this world normally operates, the greatest in the Kingdom of Heaven are those who are like little children. In God's Kingdom, there is great rejoicing over even one seemingly worthless sheep or soul which was lost but is found.

In God's Kingdom, the King is so generous and merciful he pays the same wages to everyone no matter how long or how short they worked. Everything is backwards from what we expect. The first shall be last and the last shall be first.

This Kingdom is like a wedding feast where everyone is invited— from the lowliest to the greatest, from dirty street people who never expect to be invited, to the most finely dressed who assume they will be invited. However, beware of the seating order at this party. The greatest shall be least and the least shall be greatest, and you may get asked to move if you presume too much self-importance.

In short, the Kingdom of God does not consist of anything we could anticipate, and is not what we would ever expect. Everything is turned upside down from the world as we know it. As New Testament Jesus-scholar Marcus Borg attributed to his Catholic colleague, Dominic Crossan: The Kingdom of God is what life would be like on earth if God was king and the rulers of this world were not. It is God's justice in contrast to man's injustice.

We live in a world that loves to draw lines to make sure who is included and who is excluded. We live under the false illusion that we actually own some part of this world as our private property. Think about some of the religiously motivated geopolitical lines that have been drawn in the world. The Mason-Dixon Line separating slave states and free; Northern Ireland separating Protestant and Catholic; the former Yugoslavia / Kosovo with Serbs, Croats, Albanians, and Macedonians all killing each other; Iraq, Iran, and Saudi Arabia each attempting to partition Sunnis, Shiites, and Kurds.

Christians have been no better at drawing lines between orthodoxy and nonorthodoxy. Church history demonstrates a willingness of Christians to execute fellow Christians by drowning or fire or choking or other forms of violent torture over disputable issues such as baptism. The great irony being Jesus apparently intended baptism to be a shared unifying experience of all his followers.

We obviously are not qualified to draw the lines on the Kingdom of God. In the first place, it's not our prerogative to decide who is included and who is excluded. In the second place, history proves we are not smart enough or wise enough. Thirdly, we tend to draw lines with doctrines and interpretations to determine who is out, while God wants everyone in and not one to perish. After all, it's God's Kingdom, not ours.

Citizenship in God's Kingdom is a privilege granted by the King, not a right anyone has earned or can demand. I love the sign I'm told was posted on the office door of the Special Forces chaplain at Fort

Bragg, NC: *"You are Special! Just like everybody else!"* That is what citizenship in the Kingdom of God is like.

In the Spring of 1989—as the result of a scheduling mix-up in the downtown Arena in San Antonio—at the last minute, Trinity Baptist Church ended up hosting the International Evangelism and Missions Conference of the World Council of Churches. Baptists have not been noted as participants in the World Council of Churches, and Trinity Baptist received lots of criticism from Baptist brethren.

As the associate pastor, I wasn't too pleased, either. I would have much preferred to be at the Arena watching the San Antonio Spurs and "The Admiral" David Robinson playing against the Los Angeles Lakers and Magic Johnson. That was the unlikely event that created the scheduling mix-up. But I doubt that game would have been nearly as memorable as what I experienced from the top row of the balcony in the Trinity Baptist Church sanctuary.

Ethnic people groups from all over the globe were packed, standing-room only, into a sanctuary that could not comfortably seat the crowd. Every people group arrived with the flag of their nation or tribe. Dozens of flags—including the Stars & Stripes—were visible on the chancel from my vantage point, but only one flag stood center stage: the Christian flag. The atmosphere was electric with excitement.

> *"The Kingdom of God has no geographic lines, no denominational lines, no racial, ethnic, or cultural lines."*

This is what I observed: The Kingdom of God on earth has no geographic lines, no denominational lines, no racial, ethnic, or cultural lines. God's Kingdom on this earth is not predominately Caucasian, neither is it dominated by western European culture. The Kingdom of God on earth is very colorful, incredibly diverse, and it sings in beautiful harmony.

The Kingdom of God on earth is not confined to one language, yet it prays with one voice: *"Our Father, Who art in heaven; hallowed be Thy name; Thy Kingdom come, Thy will be done, on earth as it is in heaven."* That night I caught a glimpse of what the Kingdom of Heaven looks and sounds like on earth. There was no overt evidence of competitiveness. All nations are equal in importance.

Perhaps another closely related reason we love to draw lines is the belief that somebody has to lose and somebody has to win, and everyone desires to be on the winning side. Is the Kingdom of God about winning? In respect to brothers and sisters in Christ who are different from one another, the Kingdom of God is not competitive. In respect to the Caesars of this world, the Kingdom of God wins!

The rejected and crucified Jesus appeared to be anything but a winner. However, the Resurrected Jesus is the ultimate winner. We do not have the Resurrected Jesus without first the Crucified Jesus. For many centuries of church history, the followers of Jesus did not look like winners in comparison to Caesar's dominion. That is why during times of persecution, Apocalyptic literature such as the Book of Revelation was written in cryptic language in order to reassure the faithful that, in the end, God's Kingdom is victorious.

For over a thousand years the tallest structure in the city of Rome was the Tower of Trajan. Emperor Trajan was one of the most cruel persecutors of Christians in Roman history. During his reign, many sincere followers of Jesus would not bend their knee to worship Caesar. Nor would they defend themselves in gladiatorial combat in the Coliseum. In the face of Christians who refused to fight, Trajan improvised and fed them to wild beasts for the entertainment of Roman audiences. Followers of Jesus certainly did not look like winners.

One thousand years later, Trajan's Tower became little more than a pedestal for a larger-than-life statue of Saint Peter. Tradition holds that Peter was crucified upside down by Emperor Nero. Yet the statue of Peter, considered to be the first Pope of the Catholic Church, stands atop Trajan's Tower as a symbol that the Church has endured while the Roman Empire has disappeared. The statue of Peter atop the highest pinnacle of Rome reminds us that the Kingdom of God towers over the mightiest kingdoms of men. The martyred Galilean fisherman stands triumphant over the greatest Roman military generals and Caesars who ever lived. As the Apocalyptic literature of Revelation foretold, the Kingdom of God wins.

Many years earlier, on a hillside in the north of Galilee, a penniless itinerant rabbi with twelve very ordinary disciples stood among the ruins of ancient idols in a place called Caesarea because Caesar-worship reigned supreme. There, of all places, this amazing man who defies all human categories asked the definitive question: Who do you say that I am?

It was Simon Peter, the disciple who frequently spoke without thinking, who proclaimed: *You are the Messiah of God.* The evidence is enormous that he did not know what being the Messiah really meant, yet Jesus proclaimed: *"And you are Peter! On this rock I will build my Church, and the gates of Hades will not prevail against it."*

> *"...we have often been better at drawing lines of exclusion rather than embracing inclusion."*

Through the two millennia that have followed, followers of Jesus have not always looked like winners by the world's standards. The most effective days for the spread of the Gospel in the history of the church have been during those times when Christians appeared to be losing. Neither have we been very good at drawing lines around the Kingdom of God. Much to our shame and to the detriment of the Gospel, we have often been better at drawing lines of exclusion rather than embracing inclusion.

Yet, there is one line that each and every follower of Jesus must draw. This is the one and only line that we cannot help but draw. It is a very personal line which runs down the center of your very being. Each of us stands on one side of this line

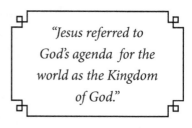

"Jesus referred to God's agenda for the world as the Kingdom of God."

or the other. On one side of the line it says: *Jesus Christ is Lord.* On the other side of the line it may say: *Caesar is Lord* (whatever Caesar may mean in each person's context). Or more likely, the other side of the line may say: *I AM LORD of my life!*

Jesus instructed us to pray in agreement with God's agenda for the world, not our personal agenda or any national agenda. He called that agenda the Kingdom of God and it supersedes all other kingdoms and agendas. It was the central theme of Jesus' preaching and the focal point of his parables. It is the central petition of Our LORD's Prayer: THY KINGDOM COME!

A most important teachable moment for citizens of God's Kingdom.

For Personal Reflection or Group Interaction

How would you describe the Kingdom of God on earth today?

How would you describe a Kingdom citizen in today's world?

In your view of the world right now, do Christians and the Kingdom of God appear to be winning or losing? Why do you think that?

Historically, Christians have been both persecuted and persecutors. What are modern-day dangers of persecution? Modern-day dangers of being persecutors?

This, then, is how you should pray:
"'Our Father in heaven,
hallowed be your name,
your kingdom come, your will be done,
on earth as it is in heaven.
THE GOSPEL ACCORDING TO MATTHEW
chapter 6 verses 9–10

In the same way
your Father in heaven is not willing
that any of these little ones should perish.
THE GOSPEL ACCORDING TO MATTHEW
chapter18 verse14

Going a little farther, he fell
with his face to the ground and prayed,
"My Father, if it is possible,
may this cup be taken from me.
Yet not as I will, but as you will."
THE GOSPEL ACCORDING TO MATTHEW
chapter 26 verse 39

And *we know* that in all things
God works for the good
of those who love him,
who have been called
according to his purpose.
THE LETTER OF PAUL TO THE ROMANS
chapter 8 verse 28

VII

THY WILL BE DONE

S omewhere, I cannot recall where, I either heard or read this humor-
ous account of a tourist to Jerusalem who observed an orthodox
rabbi praying at the Wailing Wall. The old man was dressed all in black
with a wide-brimmed hat and ringlets in his hair rocking back and
forth, beating on his chest, raising his arms and face toward heaven.

The tourist inquired: "What do you pray for?"

*"I pray for my righteousness; I pray for the health and well being of
my children; I pray for the peace of the world; and especially, I pray for
the peace of Jerusalem."*

"Are your prayers effective?" the tourist asked.

"It's like talking to a wall."

That's exactly how it can feel when praying that God's Will be done
"on earth even as it is in heaven."

Coupling *"Thy Kingdom come"* with *"Thy Will be done"* is a perfect example of the rabbinic technique of parallelism: repeating the
same idea in a different form to make it more forceful, and perhaps
clearer. In Luke's Gospel, Jesus instructed his disciples with the central

affirmation to pray *"Thy Kingdom come."* Matthew's Gospel added the parallel prayer, *"Thy Will be done, on earth as it is in heaven."*

The central affirmation of Our LORD's Prayer was made doubly clear. Followers of Jesus should desire and pray for God's agenda to be carried out in this world. Jesus intended the world we know and live in right now, not some future world.

Even before fully knowing or understanding what God's agenda for the world may be, the disciple of Jesus is instructed to pray that it should take place. If we are instructed to pray for God's agenda, then we should be equally committed to follow that agenda. No matter what it is. It is an *a priori* commitment of a sincere follower of Jesus.

If we can discern what the priorities of God's Kingdom on earth are, then as citizens of God's Kingdom and disciples of Jesus, we should adopt and follow those priorities. That's what we are doubly instructed to pray for and to do.

Simple to say. More difficult to understand. Even more difficult to do.

My suspicion is that everyone who has sought seriously to follow Jesus has at points in time struggled with the question: What is God's Will for my life? That question is felt most acutely at major turning points in life: What is my vocation to be? Where shall I go to school? Whom should I marry and spend my life with? What job should I take? Where shall we live? How much debt should we incur? The list could go on endlessly. All these questions, both big and small, are wrapped up in the larger question: What is God's Will for my life? In some respects, that question never goes away no matter how long we live.

One of the most helpful books I have ever read on this topic is *Decision Making and the Will of God: A Biblical Alternative to the*

Traditional View by Garry Friesen. This is a gross oversimplification, but Friesen describes the "traditional view" of God's Will as finding and hitting the bull's eye "dot" on a target. God's Will is a hit or miss proposition. In short, Friesen finds

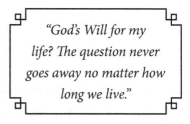

"God's Will for my life? The question never goes away no matter how long we live."

the traditional view lacking in the best biblical interpretation, and not conducive to good mental, emotional, and spiritual health. Not to mention, hitting the "dot" just doesn't seem to work in real life.

Friesen presents the traditional view of God's Will in a threefold way: God's mysterious **Sovereign Will** for all of creation, God's **Moral Will** for all of humankind, and God's **Individual Will** for each person. It's the third part that Friesen takes issue with. He sees the individual part of God's Will not as a bull's eye "dot" to be hit, but as an area of freedom inside of God's Sovereign and Moral Will. We must exercise wisdom within the area of freedom inside of God's Moral Will encompassed by God's Sovereign Will for all things.

God's Will in the area of freedom is less a blueprint or map with specific instructions and more like a compass to help us find our way. Any decision inside of God's Moral Will is acceptable, although not equally wise. In theological language, Friesen affirms both the Sovereignty of God and the freewill and responsibility of mankind. That is theologically important.

When seeking God's Will in the big decisions of life, the Moral Will of God is paramount. Is this decision fair, honest, and moral by God's standards, primarily as revealed in scripture? If not, then it cannot possibly be God's Will. That's relatively easy to know, but can still be very difficult to do. However, within the area of freedom, inside God's Moral

Will, it is difficult to know with certainty the best decision to make in any given circumstance and impossible to know the outcome.

Personally, in my own decision-making processes, seeking to know and do God's Will as best I can, I have looked for several signposts. The first signpost is *trajectory*; evidence of continuity between my past, present, and future. Nothing in the past has been wasted in the sovereignty of God. We learn and gain wisdom from our mistakes as well as our successes.

In addition to trajectory, I look for *congruence* in the parts and pieces and circumstances; how circumstances surrounding a decision may be coming together. It is often remarkable how things that are completely beyond control can point to a wise decision.

In addition to trajectory and congruence, *consensus* from trusted friends and advisors is critically important. No one is truly objective and without bias. Do friends see the same trajectory and congruence that I see? Seeking advice and taking advice are two different things. I have done both and failed to do both. Regardless of the decision made, I have always benefited by consulting friends.

Finally, I expect to have good *conscience*: to arrive at a level of comfort with the decision. Obviously there is significant subjectivity, even if wrapped in prayer and the desire to know and to do God's Will as best as can be discerned.

The truth is it is only in retrospect, looking back at any decision and its outcome, that evidence of God's Sovereign Will becomes clear. There is always the possibility that any decision may not prove out as well as hoped for. That is the inherent reality of decision-making and God's Will within the area of freedom and responsibility. It is apparently the way God has designed life to be. Even bad decisions contribute to the future trajectory of life in the sovereignty of God.

A classic contribution to the understanding of God's Will was made by Dr. Leslie Weatherhead, the long tenured pastor of City Temple in London during the first half of the twentieth century. He authored many books and was among the first pastors to combine the insights of psychology with pastoral ministry.

Known as a preacher with a positive Gospel message, Dr. Weatherhead's classic book, *The Will of God,* consisted of five sermons he preached in the bomb-damaged City Temple sanctuary near the end of World War II. His congregation had suffered many tragic losses in the Nazi firebombing of London. The casualties of war included spouses, small children, sons and daughters killed in action, and orphans left behind by parents who died. No one was untouched by the tragedy and devastation of war. City Temple was not a congregation that would accept pious platitudes about God's Will, or naiveté about God's Kingdom on earth as it is in heaven.

Although he spoke with a loving pastor's heart, Dr. Weatherhead also spoke directly to the poor theology he heard repeatedly among his parishioners. We should never, he proclaimed, attribute to God the evil that happens in this world, especially not the evil committed by men. He could not accept that Hitler and Nazism, or the results of natural calamity or disease, are the Will of God on earth.

These things, he believed, are simply not in the nature and character of God Our Father as revealed by Jesus Our LORD. God is the author of every good and perfect gift and only intends good for his children. As Jesus said, "It is *not the will of your Father in heaven that even one of the least of these should perish.*"

> "We should never attribute to God the evil that happens in this world."

Dr. Weatherhead's approach to understanding God's Will, similar to Friesen's, was in a three-fold way: God's *Intentional* Will, God's *Circumstantial* Will, and God's *Ultimate* Will. These three aspects have been for many people a helpful way of thinking about and understanding God's Will in a less-than-perfect world.

God's Intentional and Ultimate Will for this world is always only good. We can pray with bold faith that what God has *intended* from the beginning will *ultimately* take place. Humankind's sinfulness will not ultimately pervert or prevent God's Intentional Will for His creation. However, when we pray for *"God's Will to be done on earth as it is in heaven,"* we do so in the midst of God's Circumstantial Will.

Dr. Weatherhead spoke at greatest length and with greatest compassion about God's Circumstantial Will. How do we live and pray in this world that has fallen so far short of what God intended and what God ultimately desires?

I can never think about the difficulty of God's Circumstantial Will without thinking of dear friends, a single mom with a daughter who fought cystic fibrosis from three years of age. For over thirty-five years this dedicated mother rarely had a full night's sleep; her beautiful daughter *never* had a full night's sleep. This young woman spent as much of her thirty-eight years in the hospital as out of the hospital.

Together, they fought as valiantly as possible while this dreaded disease inched away at her lung capacity and her life expectancy. Drug after drug, year after year for over three decades, became ineffective as her body would build resistance to the drug's benefit with no cure in sight. She suffered through the throes of organ rejection for the final years of her life following a double lung transplant.

We dare not speak lightly of God's Will in light of such difficult suffering, just as Dr. Weatherhead dared not do so in the heart of London after World War II. Living in the midst of God's Circumstantial Will is

THY WILL BE DONE

not easy and far from perfect. Nevertheless, the apostle Paul assured us that in the midst of all things, even the evil things that may happen, we can know that God is at work for our good.

In the sometimes terrible circumstances of this world, God's Will is something that only *WE can know*. The two most important words in the apostle Paul's classic statement in Romans 8:28 are the words "*WE KNOW.*" God's Circumstantial Will is experienced in the *company of the committed, in the fellowship of believers*: in the Body of Christ on earth. *We know* the gates of Hell shall not prevail against the Kingdom of God. *We know* that God's Circumstantial Will is experienced and discovered among the greater goods and lesser evils of a world gone off track from what God intended and still desires for us.

Even Jesus in the hour of his greatest temptation and emotional pain wanted the company of his closest friends: Peter, James, and John. One of the most graphic pictures in the Bible is Jesus praying in the Garden of Gethsemane while his closest friends slept: "*Father, if it be your will, take this cup from me, but not my will, Your Will be done.*" Quaker theologian Richard Foster refers to this prayer of Jesus as "*The Prayer of Relinquishment.*" It is the supreme example of praying for God's Will on earth as it is in heaven. *Relinquish MY will, MY plans, MY desires, to God's Will.*

When we pray "*Thy will be done on earth...,*" we pray with faith, hope, and confidence that what God has intended, even though often sidetracked in the evil circumstances of this fallen world, will ultimately take place. We pray that in the midst of these often difficult circumstances, we will be for one another all that God desires us to be. For God's Will is done through *US in the fellowship of community* with one another in the midst of the difficult circumstances of this life.

From the very first word of Jesus' model prayer, we are reminded

> "It is what WE KNOW that strengthens us through the most difficult circumstances of life."

that the Creator God is not just *MY* Father, or *YOUR* Father, but *OUR* Father. It is what *WE KNOW* together that strengthens us through the most difficult circumstances of life. God's Will for the world takes place through *US* together: the Body of Christ on earth, the community of faith, the fellowship of believers, the ones who trust and hope in God.

Perhaps that is why Our LORD's Prayer has been repeated together in united voices in congregations throughout the world from the earliest days of the church until this day. We continue to pray in unison: *"Thy will be done on earth as it is in heaven."*

That is a teachable moment for all of us.

For Personal Reflection or Group Interaction

Is God's Will for your life the same or different from God's Will for every person's life?

In what ways YES? In what ways NO?

Do you subscribe more to the traditional "dot" or the area of freedom in your understanding of God's Will for your life?

How have you discerned God's Will in your life?

How do you feel God desires us to respond to suffering in life?

What is your explanation for the suffering that is in the world?

To his disciples in the upper room—Jesus said:
"Do not let your hearts be troubled.
You believe in God; believe also in me.
My Father's house has many rooms;
if that were not so, would I have told you
that I am going there to prepare a place for you?
And if I go and prepare a place for you,
I will come back and take you to be with me
that you also may be where I am."
THE GOSPEL ACCORDING TO JOHN
chapter 14 verses 1–3

To the thief on the cross beside him—Jesus said:
"Truly I tell you,
today you will be with me in paradise."
THE GOSPEL ACCORDING TO LUKE
chapter 23 verse 43

Quoting the Prophet Isaiah, the Apostle Paul wrote:
However, as it is written:
"What no eye has seen, what no ear has heard,
and what no human mind has conceived" -
the things God has prepared
for those who love him -
THE FIRST LETTER OF PAUL TO THE CORINTHIIANS
chapter 2 verse 9

The Apostle Peter wrote about
"an inheritance that can never perish, spoil or fade.
This inheritance is kept in heaven for you."
THE FIRST LETTER OF PETER
chapter 1 verse:4

VIII

AS IT IS IN HEAVEN

The opening lyrics of John Lennon's most famous recording suggest how much better off the world would be if everyone would
just imagine there was no heaven. Some refer to Lennon's *"Imagine"* as
a secular hymn, or even an atheist anthem. In fairness to Lennon, he
denied that his lyrics were antireligion. His stated position was opposition to *"my God is bigger than your god"* kind of thinking: the ultimate
basis for religiously motivated wars.

Ironically, the lyrics to *"Imagine"* describe what many would consider to be heaven on earth. No violence. No greed. No religion. No
hunger. Only peace and brotherhood as we all live as one. Those are
qualities that Jesus taught, role-modeled, and almost certainly had in
mind when he instructed us to pray for God's Kingdom and God's Will
to come on earth *"as it is in heaven."*

"Hold on! Wait a minute!" you might say. "Did Jesus teach '*no
religion*'?"

In a sense, yes. Jesus was far more concerned about relationship
with God than he was about religion. The two are not the same. Jesus

was clearly opposed to unhealthy legalistic religion that harmed people and misrepresented what God is really like. True religion is response to a loving God made known by Jesus as *Abba, Father.*

> *"Jesus was far more concerned about relationship with God than he was about religion."*

So what an irony it is that, according to Lennon, in order to have heaven, one must imagine there is no heaven. We, on the other hand, are instructed by Jesus to pray for God's Kingdom on earth to be "*as it is in heaven.*"

Dietrich Bonhoeffer, in his *Letters and Papers from Prison,* spoke of *religionless* Christianity decades before John Lennon imagined a *religionless* world. But Bonhoeffer also spoke of an *embodied* faith. My suspicion is Bonhoeffer envisioned Christianity without the baggage of institutionalism, something more pure to relationship with God as Jesus taught rather than the Towers of Babel we humans inevitably construct. Apparently, and even regretfully, our humanity makes institutional Christianity inevitable.

My friend and mentor, Dr. Buckner Fanning, frequently told his congregation: "If you ever find the perfect church, don't join it. You will ruin it." Many pastors would agree that church would be great if it wasn't for people: at least, certain people. Perhaps we are closer to wanting Lennon's religionless world and Bonhoeffer's religionless Christianity than we imagine.

Jesus taught us to pray for God's agenda to take hold on earth as it is in heaven. In Jesus' prayer, earth is analogous to heaven, not vice versa. Our prayer is for life and conduct to take place on earth as they are *already* in heaven. Earth is but a foreshadow of heaven. In a sense, according to Jesus' prayer, heaven is more real than earth itself.

C.S. Lewis wrote about heaven and afterlife in both his fiction

AS IT IS IN HEAVEN

and nonfiction works. It's almost forgotten today, but Lewis initially became well known in England not as a writer and author but as a radio program personality who talked about faith and Christianity. His most famous radio message was broadcast in 1942 at the height of the German bombing of London. It was a sermon about heaven entitled *"The Weight of Glory."*

In typical Lewis style, he argued that the natural human desire for Paradise, something far better than life as we know it, points to the existence of heaven in the same way that physical hunger points to the existence of food. Lewis was convinced that we intuit accurately that there is *something* beyond this earthly life. He then cautions against those philosophies who would limit heaven to earth, or try to convince us that this earthly life is all there is.

Lewis reminds us that all word pictures about heaven are just that: *word pictures.* All language about heaven, even biblical language about heaven, is of necessity metaphorical. Words are merely symbols of real things and actions. Words are an attempt to describe that which is real, but words are always inadequate and too imprecise to express what heaven is really like.

All language about heaven is to *ponder the imponderable.* Like a flea crawling on the back of an elephant. Can it possibly know what it is dealing with? Or like a fly flapping its wings in a tornado thinking it is creating all that wind. As the apostle Paul said: *we have never **seen**, we have never **heard**, and we cannot fully **imagine**—*what we are speaking of when we speak of heaven. Lewis concludes that the *"weight of glory"* far outweighs all the difficulties of this earthly life. In the final analysis, it is not what we say or think about heaven that counts, but what God says and means.

Peter Kreeft, a noted CS Lewis scholar and Catholic theologian, teaches philosophy of religion at Boston College. In his writing he draws heavily from a combination of scripture, Saint Augustine, Thomas Aquinas, and CS Lewis. In Kreeft's book, *Everything You Ever Wanted to Know About Heaven*, he elaborates on a concept Lewis touched on only briefly in *Mere Christianity*.

While writing about how God hears millions of prayers simultaneously, yet personally, Lewis referred to the *timelessness* of God. He grappled with the question of how God can be truly personal and yet responsive to every human being on earth simultaneously. Lewis's answer was that God is not bound by time: the linear sequence of past, present, and future. God resides *beyond time*, in the eternal present moment. Try to ponder that imponderable thought.

Imagine there is no heaven along with John Lennon? NO! Imagine the very opposite. Imagine that Heaven is very near to you this very moment, so close you can almost touch it. But because we are time-bound—heaven is *beyond* our reach.

This is one of the most fascinating concepts in the writing of CS Lewis. In fact, it is so difficult to grasp that Lewis invites readers to skip the chapter on *"Time and Beyond Time"* in *Mere Christianity* if they prefer. But Lewis was only continuing in the same vein as Saint Augustine and Thomas Aquinas long before him.

Peter Kreeft further elaborates on *timelessness* along with many theologians, philosophers, and even physicists who have proposed that there is a dimension that is beyond time. Ponder that, if you can.

"Imagine that Heaven is very near!"

Kreeft emphasizes how essential it is to use imagination when we speak of heaven and timelessness. He agrees with Lewis that words are merely *symbols*: *metaphors* that represent *images* of the reality of heaven. But words are incapable of expressing exactly what Heaven is really like because all language is analogy.

Two words in the Greek language express two different perspectives about Time. *Chronos* means the chronological passing of time from past to present to future. *Kairos* speaks of the present moment of time. We humans experience the present moment of time but cannot explain or even point to it because the present moment instantly vanishes into the past.

The material world exists in *chronos*—past, present, and future with only the fleeting experience of *kairos*, the *present moment*. Perhaps because we are created in the image of God, we are allowed to experience in the present moment a fleeting *glimpse of eternity*. Perhaps heaven is the opposite. Perhaps past and future lose their meaning in the face of the eternal present moment.

Consider this possibility. The New Testament tells us that Jesus returned to the Father to prepare a place for us, so that where He is, we may be also. If God is in timelessness, as Lewis and others have proposed, and Jesus is with God the Father, and we are going to be with Jesus; then is our heavenly destination beyond time as well?

Could it be that Heaven is to experience the eternal present with only fleeting glimpses of the past and future? Could it be that we are instantly with all those we love and have loved because the chronological sequence in which we lived and died is meaningless in heaven? Ponder that.

Consider this possibility: both the Incarnational Birth of Jesus and the Atoning Death of Jesus took place in *cosmic kairos moments in time*. The Eternal Incarnate Immanuel, *God With Us,* was born into this time-bound world in a cosmic moment in time, and He died on the cross in a cosmic moment in time, atoning for the sins of the world—past, present, and future. The eternal *kairos* invaded the temporal *chronos* and accomplished eternal redemption. That's the Good News of the Gospel at its best.

Years ago, a psychologist / therapist / friend whom I respected very much pointed out that his counseling practice could be boiled down to two things. First, helping some people move beyond the guilt of the past. Second, helping some other people move beyond the fear and anxiety of the future. He said to me: "If only I could get my clients to *live in the present* rather than the guilt of the past or the fear of the future!"

Jesus' prayer addresses that dilemma. When we pray for God's reign to take hold of our lives, and for God's Will to be done in our lives, *on earth as it is in heaven*, it is a prayer to live life in the present with neither the guilt of the past (*"forgive us our sins"*) nor the fear of the future (*"lead us not into temptation"*) in control of our present.

Throughout my years in ministry, I have repeatedly encountered what I believe to be two similar but different common misconceptions. Heaven, salvation, is contingent upon—number one, being good enough; or number two, believing the right things. Both Right Behavior and Right Belief are, in my opinion, different but similar aspects of salvation by WORKS Religion. Both depend on us, not God.

Not that we shouldn't seek to live good lives, and not that it isn't important to seek to know and believe truthful things about God. But I don't believe salvation and heaven are contingent upon either being good enough or knowing and believing correctly enough. Both of these misconceptions depend on us rather than on what God has accomplished for us in Jesus the Incarnate Word and the Atoning Sacrifice for our sins, both accomplished in cosmic kairos moments in time.

Having grown up in church, I have been fascinated by the thief on the cross from childhood. It is worth noting, no more than the cowardly disciples who fled, or the courageous women who stayed at the cross, this nameless thief knew nothing of the Incarnation of Jesus, the virgin birth, or the Trinitarian understanding of God. Neither is there any indication that he understood atonement for sin was taking place immediately next to him. He had no knowledge of the coming resurrection of Jesus from the grave or the multiple mysterious and miraculous post-death appearances of Jesus. He never heard of Jesus' ascension to heaven or His promised return in Glory.

Despite all the lack of knowledge or doctrinal belief on the part of this nameless thief—who acknowledged he was guilty as charged (hardly an admirable life) and whose only profession of faith in Jesus was a bold and desperate request to be remembered—this crucified thief is promised to be with Jesus in Paradise that very day.

Heaven is apparently not contingent on correct doctrinal belief or righteous life and behavior—but something else. Heaven has something to do with the Will of God our Father in heaven and perhaps something in the sincerity of the individual. It is not the words we say or how we say them: certainly not when or how much water we were baptized with, or even if we were baptized, but something which only God alone can see or know or determine.

My late friend, Jim Ruble, was one of the most admirable men of integrity that I have ever known. His commitment to do and speak the truth was renown among businesspeople of San Antonio and professional executives throughout the insurance industry. Following his diagnosis with incurable cancer, we talked on several occasions about the *imponderables* of heaven and the implications of CS Lewis' thoughts on the timelessness of God.

Unable to drive any longer, Jim asked me to drive him to the hospital to visit a dying friend he had led to faith in Christ years earlier. That emotional goodbye between two dying men was a memorable and meaningful experience for all three of us. On the drive home, Jim relayed to me this experience. He began, "I had a dream last night. I dreamed that I died." He instantly had my full attention.

He continued, "I had two overwhelming emotions back to back. The first was: *This is unfair! Life is too short!* The second emotion was as if God read my mind and said, *Jim, everything will be all right.*"

We drove in silence for a little while, then he said: "I have always been told that God will give us *dying grace* when the time comes." I was nodding my head in agreement when he said, "I'm here to tell you I don't have it."

I was completely caught off guard and stunned by his admission!

Then he finished: "But I am confident when the time comes, I will."

That memory of Jim's honesty about fear and faith has always helped me.

"*The most important thing we can do is try to live in the present tense.*"

Perhaps the most important thing we can do to please God and live like Jesus is to live as much as possible in the present tense; not the guilt of the past nor the fear of the future. Trusting that God our Heavenly Father through Jesus our LORD will provide each one of us with dying grace through the abiding Presence of the Holy Spirit.

Imagine there's no heaven? Not on your life!

In this teachable moment, I think Jesus would say: *Imagine heaven!* Then trust that your most vivid imagination is inadequate to the reality. Then pray that whatever you say, whatever you do, whatever you hope for or pray for here on earth would be consistent with "*as it is in heaven.*"

That is a teachable *Kairos* moment in time.

For Personal Reflection or Group Interaction

How realistic do you think it is to live on earth as it is in heaven?

Do you find the concept of timelessness in heaven to be ponderable with imagination?

Do you find the concept of timelessness in heaven to be helpful or unhelpful? Why or why not?

Do you agree or disagree that right belief is a form of WORKS religion? Why or why not?

To what degree are you able to live in the present tense?

To what degree are you in captivity to the guilt of the past?

To what degree are you frozen in place by fear of the future?

"Give us each day our daily bread."
THE GOSPEL ACCORDING TO LUKE
chapter 11 verse 3

"Give us today our daily bread."
THE GOSPEL ACCORDING TO MATTHEW
chapter 6 verse 11

"It is written: 'Man shall not live on bread alone, but on every word that comes from the mouth of God.'"
THE GOSPEL ACCORDING TO MATTHEW
chapter 4 verse 4
(The Temptations of Jesus)

"Then Jesus declared, 'I am the bread of life. Whoever comes to me will never go hungry."
THE GOSPEL ACCORDING TO JOHN
chapter 6 verse 35
(The feeding of the 5000 is the only miracle recorded in all four Gospels)

"So do not worry, saying, 'What shall we eat?' or 'What shall we drink?' or 'What shall we wear?' For the pagans run after all these things, and your heavenly Father knows that you need them. But seek first his kingdom and his righteousness, and all these things will be given to you as well. Therefore do not worry about tomorrow, for tomorrow will worry about itself."
THE GOSPEL ACCORDING TO MATTHEW
chapter 6 verses 31–34
(The Sermon on the Mount)

IX

OUR DAILY BREAD

I f it is important to live in the present rather than the guilt of the past
or the fear of the future, then the most pressing present tense need
in the world is our daily bread. This is the turning point in Our LORD's
Prayer: the transition from praying for God's Agenda for the world to
praying for our own needs in the present.

This is the only line in this most familiar prayer that Matthew's
version does not add to or elaborate on Luke's briefer version with a
parallel statement. Every other line in Luke's version is expanded in
Matthew's version except for this simple line:

"Give us this day our daily bread."

In the community where I am privileged to live, one of the most
enjoyable people I have known was Father Bob, the Paulist priest at
the Catholic Chapel across the valley from the Protestant Church
where I was pastor. When we ran into each other at social events in

the community, he would greet me in the same cheerful way: "Ahhhh … my Baptist friend!"

Father Bob was an avid tennis player well into his eighties and more than two decades my senior. He came out of retirement to lead the Catholic congregation as rector for a second time. He loved people and people loved him.

Early in our acquaintance, he invited me and another colleague to join him for lunch at his residence. He lived in a small apartment attached to the Catholic Chapel. The apartment was beautifully furnished, accentuating the view of the lake from the top of Thanksgiving Mountain.

As we sat down to partake of his attractively prepared lunch, he offered a blessing. With eyes lifted, he waved his arm at the beautiful view through the large plate glass wall and proclaimed: *"LORD, this vow of poverty is working out just great! We give Thee thanks for our daily bread."* Crossing himself, he said, *"Amen."* My colleague and I burst out laughing at the incongruity of a vow of poverty with this incredibly beautiful and affluent setting. That memorable beginning led to some lively conversation about life and ministry and resulted in a wonderful friendship.

Unlike myself, or Father Bob, the majority of the world has a primary concern: the next meal. This is the most basic human need that has not changed and may never change for the majority of the world, whether we who are affluent live with the realization or not. It is the basic need Jesus addressed in His Prayer.

That's not to say that the majority of the world is starving, although far too many are starving. It's not to say that the majority of world is going hungry, although far too many are going without adequate nutrition. It is to say that the majority of the world must give focused attention to obtaining the next meal. Even Father Bob, whose vow of poverty consisted of a meager monthly allowance, was not worried about the next meal.

The majority of the world's population does not have large kitchens with storage space, refrigerators, and freezers. Neither does the majority of the world have automobile transportation with abundant carrying capacity. Many do not live in single-family dwellings or on ground level, but must walk many miles between food and home, or up many flights of stairs. There are many and various kinds of urban and rural lifestyles in the world that are more difficult than ours, yet not considered to be poverty.

Not even considering those who are starving or who suffer malnutrition, even affluent parts of the world find it more practical to market on a daily basis and only purchase food sufficient for the evening meal and the next morning. There isn't enough storage or refrigeration space for much more than one meal and basic staples. Neither do they want to carry heavy food supplies adequate for several days.

We in the United States, unlike most of the world, have lost touch with what it means to pray *"for our daily bread."* Even the most modest Americans are affluent by the world's standards. We live in such abundance we do not know what it means to pray for our daily bread. The need of daily bread for most of the world has an immediacy that we who are affluent do not experience.

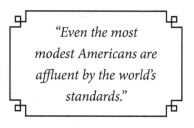

"Even the most modest Americans are affluent by the world's standards."

Our unconscious affluence was driven home to me in the 1980s when we hosted a pastor from Jamaica in our home. It was his first visit to the United States to observe and learn from us how we *"do church."* What we considered to be our modest American home was his first stop after I picked him up at the airport. We were getting acquainted standing in the kitchen as I prepared lunch for just the two of us. With a kind of innocent inquisitiveness, he pointed and asked, "What is that?"

"That's a microwave," I said. Microwaves were relatively new at the time so I was not surprised at his question. "Reheats food quickly," I explained as I continued preparing lunch without paying much attention.

"What's that?" as he pointed to our built-in double oven. At that question, I was becoming aware of his view of our *"modest American home."*

"That's an oven," I said.

"You need two?" he asked.

"We don't use both very often," I said feeling a little embarrassed. "Big holiday meals with all the family and perhaps guests." Then feeling self-conscious. "Probably not necessary, but it is not uncommon." A feeble attempt at justification.

I was cooking on the electric stove top. He pointed and asked how many "hot plates" did I have. Of course, there were four of different sizes for different cooking needs. He pointed to the toaster oven on the counter which he seemed to be familiar with, "Why do you need this?" At this point I was feeling really embarrassed at the affluence of our *"modest American home."*

"It's easier and quicker to use than heating the oven." By that point I was feeling really self-conscious of our affluence.

Then the question and the incredulous tone of voice which I have never forgotten: "Why so many?"

I had no adequate answer to our abundance of appliances that all did essentially the same thing. They helped us prepare our daily bread.

Even in our abundance, do we live with a scarcity mentality? Do we assume there is not enough to go around for all the world? Do we use that scarcity mentality as an excuse or rationale to explain away those who suffer starvation and malnutrition and other gross inequities?

Father Richard Rohr is a Franciscan priest who lives and writes in New Mexico. He has said and written on multiple occasions that scarcity is a lie: a story repeated endlessly in order to justify injustice. I don't know for certain if that's true, but what if it is? What if God has created this world abundantly capable of feeding and sustaining every single person, and only the fear of not having enough by those who have more than enough is the cause of deprivation for others?

If there really is abundance sufficient for the whole world, why are there so many in need? These questions have complicated answers about production and drought, transportation and distribution, economic systems and geopolitics. I am aware of that.

But the point is: we who are affluent are not concerned about our daily bread as the majority of people in the world today, or the people in Jesus' day. Not only do we not know what it means to pray for our daily bread, we no longer know the difference between genuine needs and unnecessary wants and desires.

> "What if the fear of not having enough by those who have more than enough is the cause of deprivation for others?"

The much larger question is: In our affluent abundance, have we lost what it means to have daily dependence on God's provision? Because our kitchen cabinets are full of food, do we assume we are not in need of God's daily provision—or do we take it for granted? Have we deluded ourselves into thinking we are really self-sufficient? That we have earned and deserve this abundant affluence we enjoy? Unconsciously, of course.

If we do not know and experience God's provision, and if we unconsciously delude ourselves into self-sufficiency rather than God-dependency, then can we really know what our needs are—as opposed to our wants and desires?

These are questions that are much larger than simply food distribution and unconscious affluence. As Jesus said, we do not live on bread alone but on every word that proceeds from God. So what does it mean for those who are affluent to depend on God for our daily bread?

In the fifteenth century, Martin Luther, in both his Longer and Shorter Catechisms on The LORD's Prayer, said *"our daily bread"* is really a metaphor for all that is necessary for life and well-being; both physical and spiritual. Luther dwelt on Jesus' understanding that our physical and spiritual needs are not divorced from one another. The way Jesus related to all people indicated he saw both physical and spiritual needs as important and essential. That's why Jesus made the point: we really do not live by bread alone.

In our self-sufficiency, asking for help does not come naturally or easily. It is an acknowledgment of our dependence upon God in the face of our obvious affluence and abundance. Asking God to supply our needs flies in the face of everything we have been taught as *self*-reliant, *self*-sufficient, *independent achiever*s who are proud of our accomplishments.

Our LORD's Prayer may have more to do with *humility* in asking than it does about our actual needs. At what points are we truly needy and dependent upon God? Philip Yancey in his book *"Prayer: Does It Make Any Difference?"* makes suggestions for those of us whose *"daily bread"* may be more subtle.

A surprising and insightful suggestion: pray for your *heart's true desires*. The honesty of admitting to God what we truly desire may humble our hearts before God and conform our desires to God's desires. Our heart's true desires may actually be closer to *"our daily bread"* than we think. Such a request may also be more like confession than request.

Another form of *"our daily bread"* may be to pray for the seemingly impossible: things we know to be impossible apart from God's intervention. Things we hope to have *"on earth as it is heaven"* such as world peace, true justice for all people, miraculous healing for those we know and love who need it.

An Old Testament prophetic thing to do is *Lament*! Make your complaints known to God. We all have them, whether we like to admit it or not. In other words, get absolutely honest with God about your inner life and desires and dissatisfactions.

Ironically, Our LORD's Prayer doesn't specifically speak of confession but it is implied. Get real and get specific about confession. Unwillingness to be on board with God's Agenda for the world is a kind of subtle dishonesty which negatively affects sincere relationship with God Our Father. Confess it! Ask for help.

In the midst of an uneasy heart and spirit, ask for personal peace and *awareness* of *God's Presence*. Even when God feels most far away. *Especially* when God feels most far away.

Ask for gratitude—especially when feeling ungrateful. Lack of gratitude is a primary indicator of self-reliance rather than God-dependence. Without gratitude, sincerely motivated generosity is unlikely. Generosity naturally follows gratitude, so pray for generosity of spirit as well as gratitude.

Ask for greater compassion for the needs of others. Lack of compassion is another indicator of self-sufficiency, or scarcity mentality, or lack of gratitude and generosity, and neglect of a reliance upon God for our daily needs and our most pressing issues.

Ask for faith in the face of doubt and lack of faith just like the man who requested of Jesus, *"Help Thou my unbelief."* There is a huge difference between faith and certainty! Certainty requires little or no faith. Uncertainty require great faith. Ask.

Whatever our true needs really are, Jesus has given us permission and even encouragement to pray for those things. That is, if in this teachable moment you can find the humility to ask with vulnerable honesty for those things that are truly—

Our Daily Bread.

For Personal Reflection or Group Interaction

What does your "daily bread" consist of?

How much of your prayers is consumed with making requests of God? Consider what you ask for most.

Now may be a good time to reconsider the way you pray. Reconsider the ACTS of prayer: Adoration, Confession, Thanksgiving, Supplication. How can your prayers for "daily bread" be improved?

*The LORD is compassionate
and gracious,
slow to anger, abounding in love.
He will not always accuse,
nor will he harbor his anger forever;
he does not treat us as our sins deserve
or repay us according to our iniquities.
For as high as the heavens
are above the earth,
so great is his love for those
who fear him;
as far as the east is from the west,
so far has he
removed our transgressions from us.*
PSALM 103 verses 8–12

*"Forgive us our sins,
for we also forgive everyone who sins
against us."*
THE GOSPEL ACCORDING
TO LUKE
chapter 11 verse 4

*"And forgive us our debts,
as we also have forgiven our debtors."*
THE GOSPEL ACCORDING
TO MATTHEW
chapter 6 verse 12

*"But whoever has been forgiven
little loves little."*
THE GOSPEL ACCORDING
TO LUKE
chapter 7 verse 47

*"Lord, how many times shall I forgive
my brother or sister
who sins against me?
Up to seven times?"
Jesus answered, "I tell you,
not seven times,
but seventy-seven times
(or seventy times seven)."*
THE GOSPEL ACCORDING
TO MATTHEW
chapter 18 verses 21–22

*"For if you forgive other people
when they sin against you,
your heavenly Father will also forgive
you. But if you do not forgive others
their sins, your Father will not forgive
your sins."*
THE GOSPEL ACCORDING
TO MATTHEW
chapter 6 verses14–15

X

FORGIVENESS

The consensus is really quite strong that living in the present tense is a spiritually and emotionally healthy practice. However, there is considerable theological debate about the future. Does God ever change His mind about the future? Or has God predetermined and fixed in place everything about the future? That debate is a bottomless barrel of disputed biblical interpretation and philosophical conjecture. But there is absolutely no debate or dispute about God's relationship to the past.

Years ago, my good buddy observed correctly that I needed to add some recreation to my overstressed life. He showed up on my doorstep and insisted that I go with him to the golf driving range near our house.

That evening he taught me the awkward, counterintuitive stance and grip that are essential to the golf swing. He persisted with me until I finally captured that sweet sound and sensation that goes with a well-hit golf shot. That was the beginning of a whole new era in my life.

Multiple evenings at the driving range and practice greens followed until he felt I was ready for my first trip to a golf course. It was a hot and humid south Texas Sunday afternoon when no one else was foolish enough to be on the golf course. On that *real* golf course, I learned the most important rule in golf: do not swing hard and do not look up to see how well you hit the ball.

Standing on the first tee box I made good contact with the ball, heard that sweet sound, and learned I had a big slice. My buddy said, "Great drive if we were playing the ninth fairway." Then for the first time I heard the most incredible phrase in fake golf: "Take a Mulligan!" So I teed up the second ball. Big hook. My buddy said, "Great drive if we were playing the eighteenth fairway." Then he said the sweetest words in fake golf: "Hit it 'til you like it." I finally made it into the correct fairway.

The second shot nestled up against a tree. I learned another valuable fake golf technique: "Use your foot wedge." I finally made it to the green and managed to get the ball in the cup. According to my buddy, "There, you see? You made a bogie. That's good." In fake golf.

At the end of my first nine holes of golf, with his creative score keeping, my good buddy said, "Great! You shot a 48 on your first outing. If we played eighteen holes, that's shooting in the nineties. Very respectable. You're ready to go out on the golf course for real." Little did I know.

Imagine my surprise the first time I went out on the golf course with my neighbor without my buddy as scorekeeper. I learned I was shooting greater than 100. On nine holes. That's when I learned the first lesson of *real* golf: there are no Mulligan's in real golf. We don't use a foot wedge and we don't get *"do-overs"!* The first rule of real golf is—*"You gotta play it where it lies."*

That is also the story of life as we know it. The past never changes: there are no Mulligans or *do-overs* in real life. The consequences remain in place no matter how great the regret. God either cannot or will not change anything about the past. At least, to this point God has never changed anything in the past. The past is fixed and nonnegotiable. Both the present and the future are subservient to the consequences of the past which will not change. That is the irreversible reality of chronological time as we know it. That is why forgiveness is essential. Life without forgiveness is untenable. Forgiveness makes the consequences of the past bearable.

Jesus knew we needed forgiveness and He knew that God Our Father had provided it from the beginning. Check out the first three chapters of the Book of Genesis. God has been forgiving and redeeming from the very beginning of humankind. Nothing has changed. Not our need. Not God's forgiving nature.

Jesus instructed us to pray for forgiveness because the very act of asking for forgiveness is confession that it is needed. Further, there is a direct connection between the experience of forgiveness and the practice of forgiveness. That is why Jesus repeatedly taught us to practice forgiveness, even forgiveness of our enemies. Forgiveness received and forgiveness offered are forever and always linked together.

Forgiveness is of Divine origin. It originated in the mind of God. We would never have thought it up or even discovered it apart from a Forgiving God. Our natural inclinations are in the opposite direction toward revenge and retribution. Forgiveness is the essential ingredient to every person's mental, physical, social, and spiritual health.

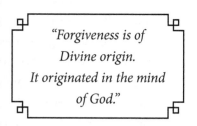

"Forgiveness is of Divine origin. It originated in the mind of God."

Forgiveness is also the essential ingredient to the healthy functioning of society and the world as we know it.

CS Lewis in his remarkable apologetic book, *The Problem of Pain,* wrote about three strands of thought he found in all developed religions, then he contends that Christianity adds a fourth unique and necessary strand not found in other religions.

The first strand is the experience of what Lewis described as the *numinous*: the uncanny feeling, belief, or experience of *"the something else*" that is beyond this physical world. For some it is an inexplicable self-awareness in the midst of random purposeless chance. But for believers it is the intentional Self-revelation of the Creator God. Regardless of the source or meaning, Lewis contends that the experience of the numinous is a universal phenomenon of humankind and that history and even prehistory bear witness to that fact.

The second strand in all developed religions is the sense of *ought-ness*. The innate evaluation that some things are fair *and* some things are unfair is a universal human phenomenon. We may disagree about *what* is fair and *what* is unfair. We may even disagree that fair and unfair represent any form of objective morality. This innate moral sensibility may be a religionless subjective morality agreed on by the cumulative experience of humankind. Or it may be an objective morality built into the very fabric of creation resulting in the religious belief in Revelation from God.

Regardless of the source, the fact that such an evaluation of fair and unfair exists is a universal human experience and one of the basic strands of all religion. There is a law of cause and effect in the moral realm as well as the physical realm. We are responsible for the freedom of our thoughts, motives, and actions. As contemplative Franciscan priest, Richard Rohr, teaches: "We are punished *by* our sins more than *for* our sins." Goodness has is its own reward. Sin carries its own consequences.

Lewis referred to the third strand found in all religions as "*the great leap.*" It is the inexplicable connection between the experience of the *numinous and* the feeling of *ought-ness* that results in the feeling of failure to meet the high standard of morality. According to Lewis, the feeling of failure to live up to the moral standard is universal. All religions are about "*closing the gap*" between the experience of the numinous and the feeling of failure to meet the moral standard.

Lewis's fourth strand is how we "*close the gap*" between the numinous and the sense of moral failure. Lewis explains that in Christianity the gap has been closed in a historical event: the life, death, resurrection, and ascension of Jesus the Anointed One of God. Eternity was effected in the cosmic *kairos* moments in chronological time when Christ entered the world and when He died for our sins.

Jesus instructs us to pray: *"Forgive us our trespasses ... our debt obligations ... our sins."* We all need forgiveness because we are all in debt and under obligation; we have all, every one of us, trespassed; we have all sinned and fallen short of God's moral standard. Something is necessary because there are no Mulligans and no *do-overs*. Nothing can change the past. We must "play it where it lies."

Forgiveness is not a Mulligan or a *do-over*. It is moving forward from where we really are, consequences included. It is playing the ball where it lies. There is no Good News about forgiveness apart from the Bad News about sin and failure. That is the Gospel story as it really is.

> *"Forgiveness is moving forward from where we are, consequences included."*

There is an apparent word confusion in Our LORD's Prayer. Perhaps you are from a tradition that prays *"forgive us our trespasses"* rather than *"forgive us our debts."* New Testament scholar William Barclay explains the seeming discrepancy:

Jesus spoke in the Aramaic language and would have verbally used the Aramaic word for **sin**. Luke's Gospel was written in Greek and used the most common Greek word for **sin**. Matthew's Gospel was composed in the Rabbinic Hebrew tradition and used the word for **sin** translated *debt* or *obligation*. William Tyndale, in the first English translation of the Bible, used the old English word *trespasses* which has survived by tradition in English.

Do not be confused. Regardless of the word used, this prayer is confession of our **sin** and admission of our need of forgiveness! In the apostle John's first letter he speaks with great clarity: *"If we claim to be without sin, we deceive ourselves and the truth is not in us."* (1:8) Then John continues with the alternative: *"If we confess our sins, he is faithful and just and will forgive us our sins and purify us from all unrighteousness."* (1:9)

William Barclay was correct when he wrote: "The greatest of sins is to be conscious of no sin." Only a narcissistic sociopath believes there is no need of forgiveness. Barclay tells the story of John Wesley in conversation with a famous British military officer who declared: "I never forgive!" To which Wesley replied, "Then I hope, sir, you never sin." There is a necessary connection between forgiveness received and forgiveness extended to others.

There is also some confusion in the two texts from Luke and Matthew about the connection between forgiveness received and forgiveness offered. The connection is clearly present, but there is an apparent chicken and egg dilemma in the two versions of Our LORD's Prayer. Jesus could not be clearer in this prayer, or in his parables, that forgiveness received is contingent on forgiveness extended. But which comes first? Our repentance or God's forgiveness? Is God's forgiveness of us contingent upon our forgiveness of others?

It is a good time to recall the illustration of the ringing cell phone. Do we call God, putting God at our disposal? Or is God constantly calling us? Who beckons to whom? Who is in the initiative? Us or God?

God is always in the initiative to redeem and forgive. We, on the other hand, are always in need of redemption and forgiveness. The biblical story is that forgiveness begins with God.

We are all like the Prodigal son in Jesus' greatest parable. Jesus draws the radical word-picture of the Creator God as a Loving Father, and as theologian N.T. Wright describes, a Loving Father who abandons his dignity and runs to welcome His wayward child home. It is the shockingly graphic picture of redemption and forgiveness running toward the wayward sinful repentant prodigal child.

The tragic fact of human nature is that we would never have invented forgiveness. On the contrary. We repeatedly invent the endless cycle of revenge which can only be broken when we respond to God's initiative of forgiveness. The Church is a forgiving community intended to practice the quality of forgiveness we pray about so casually every week in worship.

Barclay states the unmistakable significance of forgiveness: we are never more like God than when we extend forgiveness to those who have sinned against us. Reciprocal forgiveness—received and extended—is God's agenda for the world.

Nothing about forgiveness is easy. It wasn't easy for Jesus to forgive his tormentors. It isn't easy for us to follow Jesus' example and practice forgiveness. But, apparently, forgiveness is essential to the successful functioning of this sinful world.

You may not want to do what I am about to suggest:

Bring to mind the worst occasion of your life, the one that you most wish had never happened, that you prefer to never think about or remember but you can never forget. It may be an occasion when you failed miserably, hurting yourself and/or someone you love. It is irreversible and unchangeable, a permanent moment in your past.

That is when Christ died for you!

The redeeming atoning death of Jesus was a cosmic moment in time 2,000 years ago that exploded into the future and explodes into every person's unchangeable past. God our heavenly Father knows, understands, and hears your regret and heartfelt confession, and has removed that sin as far as the east is from the west! Your sin is forgiven! The painful consequences may remain. But God has forgiven you. You are released from the guilt and shame.

But can you forgive yourself? Perhaps that is the bigger question.

Alcoholics Anonymous identified the painful but effective spiritual process that brings healing of memories, and sometimes relationships, and helps one move on with life. No Mulligans. No do-overs. Playing the ball where it lies.

Step 4 of the AA Twelve Steps is to make a searching and fearless moral inventory of wrongs committed. For an alcoholic, that can be a long list. Step 5 is to admit to God, self, and another person the exact nature of the wrongs committed. On two occasions I have had the unique privilege to hear someone's Step 5. It is a humbling experience to hear someone's life confession.

After confession to God and another human being, after making a list of persons harmed, ultimately it is time in the AA 12 Steps to make amends, if it is possible. I have also had the uncomfortable experience of having a recovering person kindly, hesitantly, but forthrightly confess the anger and resentment harbored toward me for years. He asked for my forgiveness, which seemed to me like a reversal of roles. But he insisted that he needed my forgiveness for his resentment toward me. Of course, I granted his request. Here is the double-edged healing irony.

His angry feelings of resentment were attached to an occasion when I unintentionally hurt him. He asked if I remembered the incident, which I did, but it was quite frankly only incidental to me. He then extended to me his forgiveness for the wrong I had committed. Only then did he ask me why I had done the thing that hurt him so much. I was able to explain, although my explanation was clearly inadequate, even to myself. It was a cleansing experience for both of us. He was, it seemed, released from his hurt and resentment. I was better able to understand him and offer support for his recovery.

Lewis Smedes in his classic book *Forgive and Forget* insightfully proposes that we must learn to forgive because it is impossible to forget the hurts we have received and the hurts we have caused. He acknowledges that revenge initially feels more powerful, and forgiveness initially feels powerless and weak. But forgiveness is ultimately very powerful. It is an act of courageous freedom, never compulsion.

Practicing the freedom of forgiveness begets more freedom which ultimately begets real strength of character.

Anyone would be healthier to make a moral inventory of the injuries received and the injuries inflicted on others and seek to make amends. But it is far from easy and fraught with potential pitfalls. In Smedes' book, he makes many cautionary recommendations about extending forgiveness or asking for forgiveness when there is no real repentance or confession of wrong. That is not, in his opinion, real forgiveness. It is, in effect, offering or asking someone for a Mulligan, pretending the hurt and offense never really happened.

On another occasion I was confronted in a rather public way with the abrupt question: "Have you forgiven me yet?" The fact was—I didn't know specifically what offense I was supposed to forgive. The individual who confronted me had hurt and offended many people I knew personally. I can only assume—that he assumed—I was the spokesperson for the many. That was entirely too many assumptions, too nonspecific as to myself, and fraught with too little evidence of repentance on his part.

Since he chose the public setting to confront me, I felt compelled to ask, "Forgive you for what?" He quickly deflected the question and attempted to make an amusing situation for the spectators he had chosen for our serious and hurtful history. There was no admission of wrong. Certainly no indication he desired to make amends. I was not qualified to offer forgiveness on behalf of so many people other than myself. The whole situation smacked of manipulation, not contrition, confession, or repentance.

So far as I know, since he did not answer my question but chose to make a joke of a serious situation, there remains a detrimental lack of resolution. Nonetheless, we have both moved on from those hurtful unresolved events.

Jesus drew a vivid picture in the parable of a man who was forgiven a huge debt but refused to forgive a small debt. The master in Jesus' parable was intensely unhappy with that man. Similarly, in a real-life incident recorded in the Gospels, Jesus compared an ungrateful, ungracious Pharisee with a penitent weeping prostitute. Jesus was gracious toward the penitent, sinful woman, but hard on the self-righteous Pharisee.

The essential truth of Jesus' teaching is that the forgiveness we have received from God is always greater than the forgiveness we offer to others. The other truth is that one who has been forgiven much loves much. Only people who have truly experienced forgiveness can truly practice forgiveness. There is a very real connection between forgiveness received and forgiveness extended.

The fundamental meaning of forgiveness is to *"let go."* To receive forgiveness is to *"let go"* of the guilt and the shame attached to life's failures which we cannot change or forget. Forgiveness received is the key to the Kingdom of God on earth. To extend forgiveness to someone else is to turn the key we have received and unlock the Kingdom of God on earth as it is in heaven. Forgiveness begets forgiveness and creates freedom. It is possible to "let go" of the past.

When we are forgiven, we let go of the captivity of the past and are set free. The alternative is to be trapped in a negative, self-destructive, endless cycle of guilt, blame, and even revenge.

Smedes contends realistically that forgiveness does not come all at once or easily. Practically speaking, letting go does not come instantly but often comes slowly over time with repetition. We often have to let go of the same hurtful memory and forgive many times. We may have to let go and forgive without reaching a full resolution or full understanding of everything that happened to cause the hurt.

Forgiveness does not always produce reconciliation with the other person involved. Nonetheless, it is possible, over time to let go, to be set free, and open the possibility of reconciliation to the other person.

The closest we ever come to exhibiting the character of God is when we forgive. Failing to forgive, we ultimately destroy ourselves. Retaliation and revenge are fatal. As has been famously attributed to Mohandas Gandhi: If we continue to practice *"a tooth for a tooth"* and *"an eye for an eye,"* we will ultimately be a world of *"toothless, blind people."*

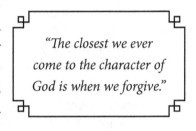

"The closest we ever come to the character of God is when we forgive."

I fondly remember the framed Chinese proverb in the office of my most admired hospital chaplain: "If in order to defeat the beast one becomes a beast, has not the beast won?" God forbid that followers of Jesus should become the beast.

In God's Kingdom on earth as it is in heaven, forgiveness always trumps revenge! A teachable moment the world has yet to learn.

For Personal Reflection or Group Interaction

What has been the most dramatic experience in your life of the reality that the past never changes?

Have you experienced CS Lewis' three strands of religion: the *numinous, ought-ness,* and *sense of failure*? In what ways?

When did Christ die for you?

Is there someone you have been unable to forgive?

The devil led him to Jerusalem and had him stand on the highest point of the temple. "If you are the Son of God," he said, "throw yourself down from here." For it is written:

"'He will command his angels concerning you to guard you carefully; they will lift you up in their hands, so that you will not strike your foot against a stone.'" Jesus answered, "It is said: 'Do not put the Lord your God to the test.'" When the devil had finished all this tempting, he left him until an opportune time.

THE GOSPEL ACCORDING TO LUKE

chapter 4 verses 9–13

"And lead us not into temptation."

THE GOSPEL ACCORDING TO LUKE

chapter 11 verse 4

"And lead us not into temptation, but deliver us from the evil one (or from evil)."

THE GOSPEL ACCORDING TO MATTHEW

chapter 6 verse 13

When tempted, no one should say, "God is tempting me." For God cannot be tempted by evil, nor does he tempt anyone; but each person is tempted when they are dragged away by their own evil desire and enticed.

JAMES (The brother of Jesus)

chapter 1 verses 13–14

No temptation has overtaken you except what is common to mankind. And God is faithful; he will not let you be tempted beyond what you can bear. But when you are tempted, he will also provide a way out so that you can endure it.

THE FIRST LETTER OF PAUL TO THE CORINTHIANS

chapter 10 verse 13

XI

TEMPTATION AND EVIL

In March 2013, Cardinal Jorge Mario Bergoglio of Argentina assumed leadership of the Catholic Church as Pope Francis. Since the tenth century new popes have been rechristened with a previously used name (John Paul I being the exception, combining two previously used names to create a new name). The fact that Pope Francis selected a never before used name that is so well known and even popular signaled his primary desire to remember the poor and rejected, just as his famous namesake did.

Just as the never-before-used name, Francis, came as a complete surprise, this Pope represented many surprising firsts. He is the first Jesuit pope, the first pope from the Americas, the first pope to come from the southern hemisphere, and the first pope from outside Europe since the eighth century. In a notable first gesture, he received the congratulations of his former peers standing, not seated, as was traditional custom. He has refused the ornate gold-laden Papal vestments, preferring greater simplicity like his namesake.

On his first Maundy Thursday service as Pope Francis, he went to a youth prison where he washed the feet of prisoners including two women and two Muslims. Unprecedented. Then in the most visible break with tradition, he refused to take up residence in the lavish papal apartments. He prefers to travel in a small fuel-efficient automobile rather than the papal limousine.

From the day Pope Francis assumed his responsibilities, he has confronted the need for change in attitude and approach to underserved people. His reluctance to condemn homosexuals engendered fear of liberalization and severe opposition from within the Church. Consistent with his unexpected and controversial beginning, in a recent book he proposed a change of wording to the easily misunderstood final line in The LORD's Prayer. Francis proposed a better translation of the original Greek suggesting: *"Do not let us enter into temptation."*

It is an important proposal reflecting better theology as well as a more accurate translation. According to Francis, a loving parent would never impose temptation on his children. Of course, conservatives within the Catholic Church and fundamentalists among Protestants immediately attacked the Pope for rewriting scripture.

> *"A loving parent would never impose temptation on his children."*

Decades if not centuries before Pope Francis brought attention to this issue, Greek scholars were pointing to variant textual alternatives in the manuscripts, as well as translation issues, in this controversial line of Our LORD's Prayer. New Testament commentators have always had to jump through hoops trying to explain away the uncomfortable implication that we must plead with God not to lead us into temptation.

In that effort some commentators have preferred to dwell on God *testing* His children, rather than *tempting*. The idea of God *testing* certainly has better biblical grounds than God *tempting* his children with evil.

Others scholars have grappled with the contradiction in the New Testament. The book of James, written by the brother of our LORD, could not be clearer that God is not tempted by evil nor does he tempt His children with evil. The line from Our LORD's Prayer as traditionally quoted is simply inconsistent with what we know about God from the rest of scripture.

But the larger point of this line in the prayer is critically important: temptation is a very real factor in life. As the apostle Paul said, *"There has no temptation taken you but such as is common to every person."* The writer of Hebrews proclaims that Jesus was tempted in every single way just as we are, only more so, because He never gave in to temptation.

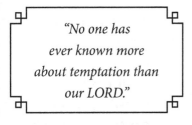

"No one has ever known more about temptation than our LORD."

Who knows more about temptation? The one who gives in or the one who resists? No one has ever known more about temptation than our LORD. We are mere amateurs when it comes to knowledge of temptation compared to Jesus. Moreover, it is unlikely that you or I have ever dealt directly or personally with the Evil One himself, as the Gospels report Jesus did.

The apostle Paul describes Satan as *"an angel of light"* appearing one way but actually being another way. Clarence Jordan's description of the devil in his creative Cotton Patch Version of the New Testament captures the idea of the satanic Evil One perfectly. He called him—the Confuser.

For many years the bestselling book by CS Lewis was *The Screwtape Letters*. In the Preface Lewis laments the love-hate relationship buyer-readers have had with this fantasy correspondence between an older, more experienced demonic Confuser named Screwtape and his young nephew, an apprentice demonic Confuser named Wormwood. *The Screwtape Letters* is a creative description of the reverse psychology of temptation at its finest (or should I say, at its worst), and a classic example of the confusing subtleties of temptation.

Lewis cautioned that there are two opposite but equal dangers regarding the devil or Satan. The first is to not take him seriously enough. The second is to dwell on him too much. If the Evil One—the devil, Lucifer, Satan, the Confuser—is an individual being and not a metaphorical personification of evil, then we need not attribute to him more power than scripture indicates. The Evil One is a created being just as we are (which begs more questions about the origin of evil without Freewill than we can enumerate).

If evil is a pervasive aspect of existence affecting everyone and everything all the time, not just a personification of evil residing in one spirit-being (a fallen angel; or minions of demonic spirit-beings), then we are dealing with something which is undeniable. Even those who claim to be atheists find it difficult, if not impossible, to deny the existence of evil while the existence of an Evil One seems farfetched.

But the scriptures do in fact personify evil in Satan—the Confuser. The better question is whether that personification is intended to be taken literally or metaphorically, or perhaps both/and. The apostle Paul seems to leave the door open when he concludes in his letter to the Ephesians: *"Our struggle is not against flesh and blood, but against the rulers, against the authorities, against the powers of this dark world and against the spiritual forces of evil in the heavenly realms."* That description is open to either possibility.

The Confuser as portrayed in scripture is obviously not Godlike in character, but neither is he Godlike in capabilities. Although a spirit-being, the Confuser does not possess the omni-characteristics of Deity. Among omni-characteristics attributable only to God, the

Confuser is *not* omniscient, knowing all things, and he is *not* omnipresent. He can only be in one place at a time, capable of tempting only one person at a time.

Of the billions of people on earth, who is the Confuser most likely to select for his personal attention? My guess would be the most powerful and influential individuals on earth who have the greatest impact on the world. Those most powerful individuals hopefully have the strongest moral character, hopefully accustomed to resisting temptation, not giving in to evil easily or frequently.

Immediately after Jesus' baptism, all three synoptic Gospels record his forty days of temptations in the Judean wilderness. Alone with the Confuser, Jesus is tempted to doubt what God has told him at His baptism: *"You are my Son in whom I am well pleased."* Each of the temptations begins with: *"IF you are the Son of God…,"* then proceeds to appeal to some very real and even legitimate human desire, such as hunger. The far greater temptation was to doubt what God had said.

From the very beginning of the biblical story, the Confuser misused and misquoted the words of God to mislead and create doubt in what God has said. He questioned Eve: *"Did God really say…?"* Of course, he misquoted what God had really said. When Jesus was being tempted in the wilderness, he answered the Confuser's temptations by quoting scripture. But the Confuser also quoted scripture to justify himself: *"For it is written…."*

When Jesus was teaching, he understood how the Confuser has always abused scriptures to mislead God's people. Jesus began a series of his teachings in the Sermon on the Mount with the phrase: *"You have heard it said…"* and quoted scripture in the way it had been misused for generations. Then Jesus responded: *"But I say to you…"* and gave the fuller more demanding meaning of what God had always intended.

One of the most critical and detrimental temptations in the

corporate evangelical Christian enterprise of today is the role of the Bible. Bibliolatry is elevating scripture as equal to the Revelation of God in creation, and equal to Jesus Himself, the Incarnate Word of God. The Bible makes no such claim for itself.

Bibliolatry is a subtle but dangerous temptation to take the written record of God's Revelation in history and deify it through literalism and inerrancy theories. That is the very kind of subtle, confusing, faith-testing temptation the Confuser uses to divide God's people and destroy our witness in the watching world.

Contrary to what many inerrancy proponents say (and some neglect to practice), the word and spirit of Jesus should always be the final criteria for interpreting and applying scripture to our lives. Scripture apart from the mind, spirit, and motives of Jesus can be easily abused and misleading. The *"angel of light"* Confuser wants us to embrace legalisms that abandon the spirit of Jesus in our relationships, especially with those we consider different or outsiders. Pope Francis is right in his Jesus-like compassion for the poor and those we consider outsiders.

We want temptation to be simple and straightforward. We want issues to be black and white with no shades of gray. We read the story of Jesus' temptations in the three synoptic Gospels and want to consider it done and over. Jesus won over those specific temptations and that was the end of it. However, a closer reading suggests that was just the beginning of temptation in Jesus' life.

The final line in the temptation story (which must have been told by Jesus Himself because no one else was present to witness it) states the very opposite. When the Confuser had failed in his temptations of Jesus in the wilderness, he left him until *"a more opportune time."*

Any time is an opportune time for the Confuser. Temptation can come through an enemy or a friend. Perhaps the most difficult to confront temptation requires a stern rebuke to someone who is loved: "Get behind me, Satan!" That is what Jesus said to his friend, Simon Peter, who tried to convince him that the way of the Messiah was not the way of the cross. Peter was unknowingly endorsing the most constant, difficult, and critical temptation in Jesus' life! The temptation to take a shortcut around the cross was the most critical, repeated temptation in Jesus' life.

The shortcut around the cross would have been the end result to any of the Confuser's desert temptations. When Jesus was on the cross, he was taunted with the possibility of calling down angels from heaven to rescue Him. That's exactly what the Confuser had suggested three years earlier in the desert. The first temptation in the desert had come full circle in the final temptation on the cross.

The 1988 award-winning movie and box office failure, "*The Last Temptation of Christ,*" was a very controversial adaptation of the 1955 Nikos Kazantzakos novel by the same name. Many Christians were outraged that Jesus was portrayed as having sexual temptations. If Jesus did not have sexual temptations, then the writer of Hebrews was in error; Jesus was not tempted in every way just as we are.

The climactic point of the movie is the last temptation of Jesus while on the cross. The temptation is not really about sex, although that has been the most severe criticism of this graphic movie. The final temptation of Jesus was to reject the role of the Messiah who must die on the cross for the sins of the world. The temptation was to love a woman, to marry, to have a family and enjoy all the pleasures of humanity and family life. The last temptation was simply to be an ordinary man, husband, and father rather than the Messiah.

Perhaps Kazantzakos captured in his novel the greatest irony of all. Our most basic temptation, the one that the Confuser used to deceive Eve in the Garden of Eden, was *to be like God* knowing both good and evil. If Kazantzakos is correct in his fictional insight, the most devastating "*angel of light"* confusing temptation of Jesus was *to be like us,* enjoying all the joys and the sorrows of this earthly life. What a paradoxical irony that is.

Contrary to what many assume, temptation may be evidence of strength, not weakness. After all, Jesus was tempted. Resisting tempta-tion builds spiritual character and strength. The greater danger is to never suffer temp-tation. As James, the brother of our LORD, said so eloquently, we are capable of being carried away by our own evil desires. No temptation from the Confuser is necessary. We are responsible for the freedom of our own thoughts, motives, and actions.

> *"Temptation may be evidence of strength, not weakness."*

One of the seductive and destructive temptations we face is to demo-nize anyone with whom we disagree, to personify evil in another person. Demonizing impugns the motives of the other person, not just the posi-tions they hold. Demonizing opponents in order to win at any cost has always been, and continues to be, the chief temptation of politics in our nation. We citizens fall prey to the techniques of demonization and our nation reaps the devastating results of giving in to that temptation.

The most subtle but effective temptation is to always focus on the evil in others rather than identify, avoid, and resist the evil within one's self, which is the focus of Our LORD's Prayer as Pope Francis suggests: *"Do not let us enter into temptation."*

I doubt seriously that Pope Francis' recommendation about the wording of Our LORD's Prayer will catch on, at least not in English language practice. We are far too captive to familiar words. The habit with which we repeat Our LORD's Prayer is too strong. However, Pope Francis' point is well taken: God does not, has not, nor will He ever lead us into temptation. It is contrary to His Nature.

The apostle Paul's advice is to avoid situations that are fraught with temptation, and when tempted, look for a way of escape which God will provide. But identifying what is evil is not as easy as we may think. Temptation is misleading and can be very subtle. It can be paradoxical. It is definitely repetitive. It doesn't just go away, but keeps returning. We must resist it over and over. Temptation is definitely confusing.

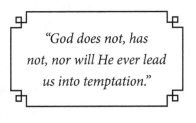

"God does not, has not, nor will He ever lead us into temptation."

Thus, the critical importance of the final petition of Our LORD's Prayer: *"Do not let us enter into temptation, but deliver us from evil."* A repetitive teachable moment.

For Personal Reflection or Group Interaction

How do you respond to Pope Francis' translation of the last line of Our LORD's Prayer? Do you think the wording can change in corporate prayer? Does it matter?

How do you perceive evil? Personified in one individual satanic Confuser? Or a more pervasive state of existence? Or some of both?

How do you perceive of the power of Satan? What are Satan's characteristics? Do you consider Satan to be literal or metaphorical?

How do you respond to the author's contention that bibliolatry is a major temptation of the church? Do you consider the Bible to be Revelation of God or the record of God's Revelation in history? What difference does that distinction make?

What is the danger or temptation of considering the mind and motives of Jesus as the final criteria for interpreting scripture? What is the danger of *not* considering Jesus as the final criteria for interpreting scripture? Can you give examples?

How can we avoid the temptation to demonize people with whom we disagree?

David praised the LORD in the presence
of the whole assembly, saying,
"Praise be to you, LORD,
the God of our father Israel,
from everlasting to everlasting.
Yours, LORD, is the greatness
and the power and the glory
and the majesty and the splendor,
for everything in heaven and earth is yours.
Yours LORD is the kingdom;
you are exalted as head over all."
1 CHRONICLES
chapter 29 verses 10–11

And do not pray as the hypocrites,
but as the Lord commanded in his Gospel, pray thus:
"Our Father, who art in Heaven,
hallowed be thy Name,
thy Kingdom come,
thy will be done,
as in Heaven so also upon earth;
give us today our daily bread,
and forgive us our debt as we forgive our debtors,
and lead us not into trial,
but deliver us from the Evil One,
for Thine is the power and the glory forever."
Pray thus three times a day.
DIDACHE
chapter 8

XII

THE DOXOLOGY

G rowing up in Mississippi in the 1950s and 60s, it was expected that the entire family gather around the table for supper every evening and on Sunday for lunch. Ours was a long narrow table created by my mother from a solid wood door purchased at the hardware store along with metal legs which she and I attached with a hand-cranked drill and a screw driver.

The entire family squeezed into an incredibly narrow space around that long narrow table. It could be very tight seating with Mother and Daddy at each end, five children, my mother's mother who lived with us, and often a guest or even two from any number of our childhood friends, cousins, or neighbors.

As an important part of the mealtime ritual, once everyone was squeezed in around the table, Mother would say: "Daddy, return *Thanks.*" We didn't say *Grace* back in Mississippi. I'm not sure we had ever heard of *Grace.*

My dad would *"Return Thanks"* in his very best King James English.

It was always the same words, said at the same cadence with the same inflection, or lack of:

We give Thee thanks
for these our many blessings
to the nourishment of our bodies
and thus to Thy service."

There would be a very brief pause and then the *grab session* would begin. That is what my sister's friend Jenny, who was an only child, called it. It's not that my mother didn't teach us good manners; we were just impossible to control.

Note that my dad's prayer never had an "Amen." There was no formal ending to his blessing offered for our meal. I always wondered why, but never asked. There was always a brief pause, as if we were not sure if something would come next. And it never did. Then we began to grab the food.

That's much the way Our LORD's Prayer ends in the Gospel accounts. It just ends. We can only surmise that is why, as the years and decades went by, numerous Doxologies were added to the prayer until, finally, we have the Doxology that Protestants commonly use today by tradition:

"For Thine is the Kingdom, and the power,
and the glory forever. Amen."

One of those hard-to-explain ironies is that Catholics, who refer to Our LORD's Prayer as the *"Our Father,"* follow the pattern of Matthew's Gospel and do not include the final lines of the Doxology. We Protestants, who proudly assert *Solo Scriptura* without the hindrance or benefit of authoritative tradition, include the nonbiblical Doxology. Logic would have predicted opposite roles in regard to the Doxology, but such is the strength and power of traditions.

The word "Doxology" is taken from two Greek words for *glory* and *word*. Doxology means *"word of glory"* and most often is a short hymn of praise to God used in worship services. Doxologies were often sung at the end of public prayer. The tradition originated from the Jewish synagogue and carried over into the early first-century worship in churches.

Although there are numerous versions of the Doxology to Our LORD's Prayer in early manuscripts of Matthew's Gospel, most scholars do not consider it part of the original text of Matthew. Most modern translations do not include it in the main body of the text but mention it only in footnotes. The early second-century document, *The Didache,* includes an early form of the Doxology which the better manuscripts of Matthew exclude.

Many biblical scholars conclude that this Doxology was derived from the prayer of praise found in I Chronicles 29 when King David dedicated all the materials to be used by his son, Solomon, in the construction of the First Temple.

Although Protestants include this Doxology as a routine traditional part of Our LORD's Prayer, it was originally more like a spontaneous resounding response, often sung, that the people would add to the end of the prayer. It was an exclamation of praise, a vocal pledge of allegiance to God's Kingdom agenda, added onto the end of the prayer. It is not difficult to imagine the higher volume declaration tacked onto the end of the prayer: *"For Thine is the kingdom, and the power, and the glory forever."*

In the first, second, and third centuries these words, spoken with

> "The Doxology challenges forever the true meaning of earthly kingdom, earthly power, and earthly glory."

such declarative power, were risky and dangerous. These words challenged the one world kingdom of Rome, threatened the greatest political and military power of Rome, and flew in the face of the preeminent glory of Rome. The Doxology to Our LORD's Prayer challenged forever the true meaning of earthly kingdom, earthly power, and earthly glory.

Just as followers of Jesus in those early centuries confronted the terrible dilemma of allegiance to God's Kingdom and also an earthly kingdom, so do followers of Jesus in our own day.

One of the great privileges of my life has been to travel on two occasions to the other side of the earth to teach young pastors in Irkutsk, Siberia. It was in the mid-to-late 90s shortly following the collapse of the Soviet Union. My inquisitive pastoral students asked many questions, not just about the biblical and theological subject matter we studied, but about our churches and Christian practices in America.

They had heard many rumors about our country and our ways of life. They asked about my family, house, cars, income, the size of our churches, and many other facets of American life. One of their many questions regarded the rumor that churches in America posted the American flag in our houses of worship. In their experience, it was unthinkable that this was a voluntary, noncoerced practice. Knowing at least a little about their history and background, it was not difficult to understand their shock and dismay at my answer.

These Russian students understood, in a way that we in America do not, the difficult dilemma between the Kingdom of God and the kingdoms of this world. They understood clearly that no earthly nation, including the Russian Federation or the United States, is even remotely equivalent to the Kingdom of God.

The Kingdom of God was the focus and message of Jesus in word and deed and in the prayer that he taught us. It is a disservice to the Gospel if we demote God's Kingdom in relation to any particular nationalism. This is a not so subtle temptation in the practices of Christian citizens and churches today.

Ironically, Christians in nations we consider to be adversarial, such as Russia, seem to understand this Kingdom principle better than we do. Christians in Russia, whether Orthodox, Protestant, or Catholic, would never consider displaying a Russian national flag in their houses of worship. They know all too well there is no equivalency between their nation and God's Kingdom.

We, on the other hand, justify noncoercive patriotic practices in our churches because our constitution guarantees liberty of conscience and freedom of worship. That may be permissible because it is noncoerced, but far too many fail to grasp the subtle but significant difference between patriotism and nationalism.

Perhaps this Doxology became part of Our LORD's Prayer because it is such a constant temptation to forget which Kingdom deserves our *first* allegiance. Which source of power actually fuels our lives? Whose glory are we to seek and how are we to seek it? It is an ever-present temptation to pledge our first allegiance to this world's kingdoms rather than the Kingdom of God on earth as it is in heaven.

What a powerful statement it would be if every time we repeat the words to this all too familiar prayer, the prayer which was first spoken from the lips of Jesus Himself; which was remembered, repeated, and transmitted by his first disciples; which has been cherished and passed forward from generation to generation for over 2000 years; which is still repeated every week in congregations from every nation around the earth in every language known to mankind....

What a powerful statement it would be if the Doxology to Our LORD's Prayer was exclaimed in loud victorious voices raised in unison to pledge our first allegiance—

For Thine is the KINGDOM
And the POWER
And the GLORY
FOREVER !
AMEN.

For Personal Reflection or Group Interaction

When you think of Christians in countries which are our traditional adversaries (such as Russia, China, Cuba, Iran, or Iraq), which allegiance would you prefer those Christians pledged to first—the Kingdom of God or their nation? Why?

To which Kingdom do you pledge your first allegiance? Is this a challenging question for you? Why or why not?

What is the difference between patriotism and nationalism?

How do you feel about displaying our national flag in our houses of worship? If it is a practice in your church, how do you feel it is justified?

Finally the temple guards went back
to the chief priests and the Pharisees,
who asked them,
"Why didn't you bring him in?"

*"No one ever spoke
the way this man does,"*
the guards replied.
THE GOSPEL ACCORDING TO JOHN
chapter 7 verses 45–46

POSTLUDE

WHAT KIND OF JESUS?

O ccasionally someone will ask me how much time I spent study-
ing and preparing a particular sermon. Often my answer is "All
my life." Granted, I spent a number of hours over several days preparing that particular sermon. But it is also true that it was the end result
of all my life experience on that subject up to that point.

There is a sense in which I have been writing this book all my life.
But I also preached a series of sermons on The LORD's Prayer in 2007
and numerous other related sermons over the years that became the
launching pad for each chapter. But it is also true that I began editing
and rewriting in earnest in early 2018.

In early 2018, we were in the aftermath of another high-profile
mass shooting. The students from Marjory Stoneman Douglas High
School in Parkland, Florida, chose to not be silent. One year later, students and parents are still demanding action from governments, both
state and national, and are attempting to hold elected officials account-
able. Tragically, in early 2019 two of those students have committed
suicide.

Entering the fourth quarter of 2018 there was yet another high-profile mass shooting at the Tree of Life Synagogue in Pittsburgh, Pennsylvania. Schools, churches, and synagogues are by nature the most defenseless locations in the world. Persons made hateful by mental illness or made mentally ill by hate are an inherent danger in an unprecedented way. People from around the world, as well as here in the US, have been asking: What is happening in our culture to bring this about?

One of the standard recommendations to end gun violence in America is to arm more good people with guns for protection. That is the logical response for those whose desire is to own or sell more guns. But what should be the logical response for those who are followers of Jesus? How I wish the answer to that question was clear. But, obviously, it is not.

> *"Any controversial issue, no matter how complicated, must first be boiled down to its most fundamental question."*

Years ago I came to the realization that any controversial issue, no matter how complicated, must first be boiled down to its most fundamental question. It is necessary to first identify the fundamental question in order to determine where to stand on any given issue. Then from that basic stance it is possible to respond more consistently to specific contextual situations related to the issue. If the situation warrants departing from the basic stance, at least we know we have departed from the ideal.

In 1996, a local San Antonio televangelist announced on his TV program that his church was going to have a slave auction. The idea was to auction off high school students to earn money for their summer camp. It was a bad idea from a good intention that created negative news coverage from coast to coast. The pastor-televangelist was apparently caught off guard by the firestorm of attention to his slave auction.

My friend and mentor, Buckner Fanning, made a memorable comment to me on this particular situation: "When you find yourself on the wrong side of an issue and the wrong side of history, no matter how well intended, the only solution is move to the right side of history and the right side of the issue."

Our neighboring pastor-televangelist could not defend a slave auction, no matter how naively well intentioned it had been. He had to denounce slavery and anything that smacked of racism, which he did. Their camp fund-raising effort was on the wrong side of history and the wrong side of a critical moral issue. It didn't matter what the intent had been.

The classic example of departing from the ideal is found in the life of Dietrich Bonhoeffer. An avowed Christian pacifist, Bonhoeffer participated in an assassination attempt on Adolf Hitler. He obviously felt that the extraordinary circumstances of Nazi Germany warranted a departure from his ideal. As a Christian ethicist, Bonhoeffer apparently opted for the lesser of two evils and considered it morally justified to stop the madman in a motorcar who was running over innocent pedestrians on the sidewalk. That was the justification and illustration he used.

This method of moral judgment is called methodological presumption. It is the basis of our American system of jurisprudence. We presume anyone is innocent, that is the presumption, until proven to be guilty, that is the exception. A guilty verdict must bear the moral burden of proof before departing from presumed innocence. The same principle is involved in fundamental questions for those who call ourselves Christian.

What kind of Jesus do we follow? What would Jesus do? The answer to that question should be our moral presumption as Christians. We only depart from that presumption and move to the exception if the moral burden of proof is met.

Does the Jesus you follow achieve peace through violence? That is a fundamental question. That question requires us to examine the life, message, and example of Jesus with as clear

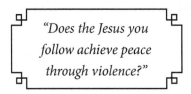

"Does the Jesus you follow achieve peace through violence?"

and unprejudiced thinking as possible. What we conclude about Jesus is the presumption that should inform our positions on critical issues. Depart from the ideals of Jesus if we must, but recognize that we are departing from the ideal and not creating a new ideal.

The presumptions we hold about Jesus will reveal the Jesus we really follow. Do we shape Jesus to fit our agendas? Or do we determine our agenda based upon what we understand about Jesus? The positions we hold will reveal the Jesus we really follow far more than the words we use on Sunday at church.

The biblical Jesus, described by the four Gospel evangelists, refused to practice self-defense. There really is no credible disagreement with that presumption. John's Gospel declared Jesus to be the Lamb of God who takes away the sins of the world through self-sacrifice. At the same time, the Jesus we see in the New Testament was never indifferent to injustice. He never turned a blind eye to evil.

Ironically, the largest portion of evil that Jesus confronted was in the self-righteous keepers of the religious status quo, not common sinners or representatives of the Roman government. We see Jesus confronting evil, changing the world to defend the innocent, upholding justice, and confronting the subtle Confuser. How can we as faithful followers of Jesus do the same?

Perhaps our teachable moment is found in church history. Jesus' most faithful early followers changed the world through a nonviolent refusal to be molded to the world of Caesar. They were as radical in

WHAT KIND OF JESUS?

nonviolence as their LORD had been. Church history is filled with examples of bold and courageous world changers who refused to bend their knee to Caesar in whatever form Caesar took.

On the other hand, our LORD's most embarrassing followers attempted to change the world through the means of Caesar. They used Crusades and Inquisitions and torture, not just on their enemies but even on fellow believers with whom they disagreed. That is the ultimate result and inevitable outcome of demonization.

As Christians, we really do have to decide what kind of Jesus we follow and join his agenda as presented in his prayer for God's Kingdom on earth as it is in heaven. The spirit and example of Jesus really is the final and fundamentally necessary criteria for interpreting the Bible and how we are to live the Christian life.

Scripture can be confusing, offering alternative opposing viewpoints. For example: Shall we join with the prophetic vision of Isaiah (chapter 2, verse 4) and *"beat our swords into plowshares, and our spears into pruning hooks"*? Or shall we join in the opposite vision of the prophet Joel (chapter 3, verse 10) and *"beat our plowshares into swords and our pruning hooks into spears"*?

Isaiah finished his prophecy with *"neither shall they learn war anymore."* (2:4) Joel finished his prophecy with *"let the weak say, I am strong."* (3:10) Two different Old Testament prophets, two diametrically opposite biblical visions of the world, two entirely different outcomes. Which is it? Which is the Biblical worldview?

Apparently, we have to choose.

When we gather in worship each Sunday and repeat the words to Our LORD's Prayer, we are confronted: What vision of the world did Jesus have? What was his agenda for the world? What kind of followers

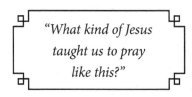

"What kind of Jesus taught us to pray like this?"

did he train and what did he teach them? What kind of Jesus taught us to pray like this?

This familiar prayer which our LORD taught tells us what kind of Jesus He really was. This modest effort is far from an exhaustive examination of Our LORD's Prayer. We will never get finished finding teachable moments from the most familiar prayer in the world. It is a lifelong lesson in praying for the agenda of Jesus for the world.

Recognize the Creator God as your Heavenly Father. He has dialed your number, the cell phone is ringing, He is waiting for you to answer.

Honor His Name. His reputation will depend on your conduct. The Jesus you choose to follow will make all the difference in how you honor Him.

Seek His Kingdom first. Align yourself with His Agenda for the world. God's Kingdom will ultimately prevail against all earthly kingdoms.

Pray for your daily bread, your true needs that reveal the true desires of your heart. Pray for the seemingly impossible. It may be within God's Will on earth as it is in heaven.

Confess your need of forgiveness and let go of your unchangeable past. That is *the key* to the Kingdom of Heaven.

Forgive your enemies and your loved ones who have wronged you. That *turns the key* to the Kingdom of heaven on earth.

Commit your unknown future, fraught with potential temptations, into the hands of God our Father who wants only the best for you.

Then once again, in a loud and clear voice, pledge your allegiance to the Kingdom, the Power, and the Glory of God—first and foremost.

These are presumptive Teachable Moments from the world's most familiar prayer. Depart from them only with great caution.

For Personal Reflection or Group Interaction

The author contends that in order to arrive at ethical and moral positions as Christians, we must boil down any issue to its most fundamental question and what we believe Jesus' response would be to that question. The author posed a fundamental question:

Does Jesus achieve peace through violence? Do you agree that is a fundamental question? Why or why not?

Is the answer to this question a valid presumptive position in the real world?

What other fundamental questions on major issues do you experience as a follower of Jesus?

SOURCES AND RESOURCES

Preface
WHY PRAY?

*A*ll in the Family was a ground-breaking television sitcom that dealt with a wide range of previously taboo subjects on television. It was broadcast on CBS television network for nine seasons from January 1971 to April 1979.

William James, *The Varieties of Religious Experience—A Study in Human Nature* (New York: Random House, 1902).

Blaise Pascal's quote about a *"God-shaped* vacuum in the *human heart"* is a popularized, nonliteral quote, derived from his posthumously published reflections and thoughts, *Pensees*.

Three Ancient Texts

The Holy Bible, New International Version (International Bible Society, 1973, Revision 2011).

The Didache, also known as *The Teaching of the Twelve Apostles*, is an anonymous early Christian treatise, dated by most scholars to the early second century or late first century. There are several translations available in English. The Roberts-Donaldson translation which incorporates the more familiar King James style English is selected for familiarity. www.earlychristianwritings.com

Chapter i
A TEACHABLE MOMENT

Welcome Back, Kotter was a controversial television sitcom in the 1970s due to its racially and ethnically integrated classroom setting. Recorded in front of a live studio audience, it aired on ABC from September 1975 through May 1979.

William Barclay, "The Gospel of Luke" in *The Daily Study Bible Series* (Philadelphia: The Westminster Press, Revised Edition, 1975)

Joachim Jeremias, *The Prayers of Jesus,* Section I "Abba" (Philadelphia: Fortress Press, 1967).

The Didache www.earlychristianwritings.com

Joachim Jeremias, *The Prayers of Jesus,* Section III "The Lord's Prayer in Light of Recent Research" (Philadelphia: Fortress Press, 1967).

Chapter ii
A CERTAIN PLACE

Marcus Borg, *The Heart of Christianity*, chapter eight, "Thin Places: Opening the Heart" (San Francisco: Harper Collins Publishers, 2003).

Richard Foster, *Prayer: Finding the Heart's True Home,* chapter 1, "Simple Prayer" (San Francisco: Harper Collins Publishers, 1992).

Dietrich Bonhoeffer, *The Cost of Discipleship,* chapter 15, "The Hiddenness of Prayer" (New York: The MacMillan Company, 1937, 1963).

Chapter iii
WHAT GOD IS NOT LIKE

William Barclay, "The Gospel of Luke" in *The Daily Study Bible Series* (Philadelphia: The Westminster Press, Revised Edition, 1975)
"The Poem of the Unknown Confederate Soldier" is anonymous and apocryphal and readily available on the internet without reliable documentation or verification.

Chapter iv
OUR FATHER

James W. Fowler, *Faithful Change: The Personal and Public Challenges of Postmodern Life,* chapter 2, "Stages of Faith and Emotions" (Nashville: Abingdon Press, 1996).
G.K. Chesterton is quoted by so many and so frequently that some quotes have taken on a life of their own. The particular wording I used is not a precise quote of Chesterton's words but quoted as often attributed to him. www.chesterton.org
Saint Augustine's famous quote is another popular saying that has taken on a life of its own. It is difficult to source and reference in the form which it is most commonly quoted, but it is derived from words used by the bishop of Hippo. www.wikiquote.org
Willard Sterne Randall, *Alexander Hamilton: A Life* (Harper Collins Publishers, 2010).

Chapter v
HALLOWED NAME

Charles Caldwell Ryrie, *A Survey of Bible Doctrine* (Chicago: Moody Press, 1972) The Hebrew and Greek words used in reference to G-d and characteristics of G-d can be found in many theological reference books. This concise but thorough book has been my starting point and departure point for theological and biblical doctrine for many years.

Chapter vi
THY KINGDOM COME

Marcus Borg, *The Heart of Christianity*, chapter seven, "The Kingdom of God: The Heart of Justice" (San Francisco: Harper Collins Publishers, 2003).

The World Council of Churches Mission and Evangelism Conference held in San Antonio in 1989 was remarkable for a consensus statement reached on the relation between Christianity and other religions: *"We cannot point to any other way of salvation than Jesus Christ; at the same time, we cannot put any limit to God's saving power. There is a tension between these affirmations which we acknowledge and cannot resolve."* www.oikoumene.org

Chapter vii
THY WILL BE DONE

Garry Friesen, *Decision Making and the Will of God: A Biblical Alternative to the Traditional View* (Portland, Oregon: Multnomah Press, 1980).

Leslie Weatherhead, *The Will of God* (Nashville: Abingdon Press, 1944, 1972).

Richard Foster, *Prayer: Finding the Heart's True Home*, Part I, chapter 5, "The Prayer of Relinquishment" (San Francisco: Harper Collins Publishers, 1992).

Chapter viii
AS IT IS IN HEAVEN

John Lennon and Yoko Ono, "Imagine" is the best-selling single of Lennon's solo career. Recorded in May 1971 in Lennon's home studio, it is one of the 100 most-performed songs of the twentieth century. It ranked number 30 of the 365 Songs of the Century bearing the most historical significance. www.wikipedia.org

Dietrich. Bonhoeffer, *Letters and Papers from Prison* (London: S.C.M. Press Fontana Books, 1953).

Buckner Fanning was the senior pastor of the Trinity Baptist Church in San Antonio, Texas, for forty-two years from 1959 until 2001. One of the most recognized people in south Texas, he was noted for his creative 30-second devotional messages on local television.

CS Lewis, *"The Weight of Glory"* was originally preached in the Church of St Mary the Virgin, Oxford, England, on June 8, 1942, and subsequently published in THEOLOGY, November, 1942. www.verber.com/stash/weight-of-glory.pdf

Peter Kreeft, *Everything You Ever Wanted to Know about Heaven ... But Never Dreamed of Asking,* chapter 10, "Is There Time in Heaven?" (San Francisco: Ignatius Press, 1990).

CS Lewis, *Mere Christianity,* Book IV, chapter 3, "Time and Beyond Time" (New York: The Macmillan Company, 1943, 1945, 1952, paperback edition 1960).

Chapter ix
OUR DAILY BREAD

Richard Rohr, *Daily Meditation from the Center for Action and Contemplation.* www.cac.org

Martin Luther, *Luther's Small Catechism on The Lord's Prayer* (St. Louis: Concordia Publishing House, 1986) www.cph.org

Phillip Yancey, *Prayer: Does It Make Any Difference?* chapter 19, "What to Pray For" (Grand Rapids, Michigan: Zondervan, 2006).

Chapter x
FORGIVENESS

CS Lewis, *The Problem of Pain*, chapter 1, "Introductory" (New York: Macmillan Publishing Company, 1940, 1962).

N.T. Wright, *The Lord and His Prayer*, chapter 4 (Grand Rapids, Michigan: William B. Eerdmans Publishing Company, 1996).

William Barclay, *The Lord's Prayer*, chapter 7, "Forgiven and Forgiving" (Louisville, Kentucky: Westminster John Knox Press, 1964, 1998).

The Twelve Steps of Alcoholics Anonymous can be found at www.aa.org

Lewis Smedes, *Forgive and Forget: Healing the Hurts We Don't Deserve* (San Francisco: HarperCollins Publishers, 1984, 1996).

Mohandas Gandhi's quote is also sometimes attributed to Martin Luther King, Jr. who quoted Gandhi without attribution. According to the *Yale Book of Quotations*, it is an authentic Gandhi quotation, but no example of its use by the Indian leader has ever been documented. www.quoteinvestigator.com

Chapter xi
TEMPTATION

Greg Carey, "Pope Francis says God doesn't lead us into temptation. What does the Bible Say?" *The Christian Century*, December 15, 2017.

CS Lewis, *The Screwtape Letters* (New York: Macmillan Publishing Company, 1961).

Clarence Jordan, *Cotton Patch Gospel: The Complete Collection* (Macon, Georgia: Smyth & Helwys Publishing, Inc., 2012).

Charles Caldwell Ryrie, *A Survey of Bible Doctrine* (Chicago: Moody Press, 1972) I agree with Ryrie's definition of *bibliolatry*, but I depart from his application of what practices are or are not idolatrous.

The Last Temptation of Christ was a critically acclaimed box office failure directed by Martin Scorsese. Roger Ebert wrote that the film-makers *"paid Christ the compliment of taking him and his message*

seriously, and they have made a film that does not turn him into a garish, emasculated image from a religious postcard. Here he is flesh and blood, struggling, questioning, asking himself and his father which is the right way, and finally, after great suffering, earning the right to say, on the cross, 'It is accomplished.'" www.wikipedia.com

Chapter xii
THE DOXOLOGY

William Barclay, *The Lord's Prayer*, final chapter "The Epilogue" (Louisville, Kentucky: Westminster John Knox Press, 1964 and 1998).

Postlude
WHAT KIND OF JESUS?

Eberhard Bethge, *Costly Grace: An Illustrated Introduction to Dietrich Bonhoeffer* (San Francisco: Harper & Row Publishers, 1976, 1979).

J. Philip Wogaman, *A Christian Method of Moral Judgment* (Philadelphia: Westminster Press, 1976).

Acknowledgments and Gratitude

Good and faithful friends read and commented on early versions of this manuscript and made invaluable suggestions and affirmations: Patricia White, Pat Coventry, Kay Herring, Linda Wilson, Jim Jorden, and Babs Baugh. Thank you once again.

Johnny White served as pastor and senior pastor of the interdenominational Protestant Church at Horseshoe Bay, Texas, for twelve years. Previously, he served for over twenty-five years in a variety of roles with married and single adults and as the senior associate pastor of Trinity Baptist Church in San Antonio, Texas. He retired from local church ministry in May 2017. **Johnny** and **Patrica** spend their time in church and community volunteer service in Horseshoe Bay where they continue to make their home—halfway between their three married children and six grandchildren who live in San Antonio and Fort Worth.

Johnny can be reached at
johnny@church-hsb.org
830-613-8386

or write in c/o
The White House of the Highland Lakes
1318 Hi Circle North
Horseshoe Bay, TX 78657